AW WITH WORDS

Young Writers' 16th Annual Poetry Competition

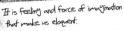
It is feeling and force of imagination that make us eloquent.

How can I not dream while writing? The blank page gives a right to dream.

YoungWriters

Norfolk

Edited by Mark Richardson

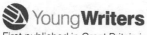 Young**Writers**

First published in Great Britain in 2007 by:
Young Writers
Remus House
Coltsfoot Drive
Peterborough
PE2 9JX
Telephone: 01733 890066
Website: www.youngwriters.co.uk

SB ISBN 978-1 84602 818 2

Foreword

This year, the Young Writers' *Away With Words* competition proudly presents a showcase of the best poetic talent selected from thousands of up-and-coming writers nationwide.

Young Writers was established in 1991 to promote the reading and writing of poetry within schools and to the young of today. Our books nurture and inspire confidence in the ability of young writers and provide a snapshot of poems written in schools and at home by budding poets of the future.

The thought, effort, imagination and hard work put into each poem impressed us all and the task of selecting poems was a difficult but nevertheless enjoyable experience.

We hope you are as pleased as we are with the final selection and that you and your family continue to be entertained with *Away With Words Norfolk* for many years to come.

Contents

Downham Market High School

Jonathan Grainger (12) 80
Daniel Tompson (12) 80
Adam Browne (12) 81
Eleanor Gash (12) 81
Verity Hemp (12) 82
Laura Butcher (12) 82
Gregory Drew (13) 83
Sam Rock (12) 83
Millie Yorke (12) 83

Hethersett Old Hall School
Ursula Denson (13) 84
Rebekah Oelrichs (11) 85
Bethany Shearing (11) 85
Ellie Davies (11) 86
Catherine O'Neill (11) 86
Rose Herbert (11) 87
Abigail Ulrych (13) 87
Hannah Gowing (12) 88
Madison-Mae Gianfrancesco (12) 88
Kim Hazell (11) 89
Hannah Gaskin (11) 89
Jasmine Philpott (13) 90
Charlotte Bacon (12) 91
Claudia Grattan (12) 92
Vicky Ramshaw (12) 93
Chloe Lochhead (12) 94
Harriet Waring (12) 95
Katie Nunney (12) 96
Francesca Warner (13) 97
Alice Baillie-Johnson (13) 98
Camilla Carr (13) 99

Litcham High School
Simon Waterfall 99
Amy Lewins (11) 100
Jernene Poponne (12) 100
Sam Bates (11) 101
Ryan Pooley (11) 101
Liam Reeve (11) 102
Conor Fraser (11) 102

The Poems

Maybe You, But Not Me

To live and not to breathe
Is to die without trying.
Who wants to try?
Maybe you, but not me.

I stand in the shadows
Where no one can see me.
Who wants to see me?
Maybe you, but not me.

I'm punched and kicked
Until I no longer feel.
Who wants to feel?
Maybe you, but not me.

I lie on my bed
Not dead but alive.
Who wants to be alive?
Maybe you, but not me.

I say to myself
I don't want to be bullied.
Who wants to be bullied?
Maybe you, but not me.

Rachel Grove (14)
Downham Market High School

My Brother's Screaming, My Sister's Crying

My brother's screaming, my sister's crying,
All the humans must be lying.
Cuts and bruises, broken bones,
From the cages come pitiful moans.
Starving hungry, dying of thirst,
What have we done to deserve this curse?
Ugly men just stand there laughing,
Not knowing the agony that they're causing.
We shout, we holler, we plead with our eyes,
We wish for help and response to our cries.
You tie us up with rusty chains
And then inject poison into our veins.
Day by day you torture us more,
We're left in agony on the floor.
Mothers, fathers, children too,
Oh, why do you treat us like you do?
Why won't you help us? What have we done wrong?
We've been left here for dead for so long.
We're there for your pleasure, we're treated like slaves,
Our only escape is our own bloody graves.

Katie Williamson (14)
Downham Market High School

I Met A Girl!

I met a girl with long blonde hair,
Lovely blue eyes, I don't care.
Her skin is soft, her skin is fair,
What am I going to do with this lovely girl here?
Buy her treats and buy her sweets,
Also take her to the ball and make her feel ten feet tall.

At the ball we will dance and sing
And then she will fly with her giant wing.
We will dance all night long
And her voice is like a blackbird's song.

Charlotte Hearle (11)
Downham Market High School

The Old Git

He used to be my best mate,
But I didn't like him much.
His eyes are as blue as the deep blue sea,
We called him a git because he didn't have a bath,
So we threw him in the wash tub
And scrubbed him red-raw.

He said he hung around with 15 mates,
But who were his mates and where did he hang around?
In the park or in the towns?
He cracks the ground as he walks,
If I stay with him any longer,
I will definitely turn into an old git.

Kai Nicholson (11)
Downham Market High School

Sunshine

Sunshine is beauty that you see,
A bright light that shines down on you and me.
It shines round every corner and every bend
And to a new season it will ascend.

Sunshine is the sound of waves on a beach
And the sound of seagulls flying overhead.
Sunshine is the smell of chocolate when it melts
And the smell of a fresh lemon tree.

It feels warm and soft, like a cuddle
When you sit next to the fire on a cold night.
When you taste, it's a burning sensation,
Something fiery and hot that burns all your troubles away.

Chloe Shade (11)
Downham Market High School

Planets

My name is the sun,
I am bright and yellow
And I am a happy fellow.

My name is Mercury,
I am as red as an alarm,
I have a special charm.

I am a special planet,
I am orange as a carrot,
I love to eat porridge.

People live in this planet,
I have a lot of sea,
I love to drink tea.

This planet is made of chocolate,
I have a creamy caramel centre,
I have an inner layer of biscuit.

Great Jupiter is my name,
I am moist and truly warm,
By nature I can do harm.

I have rings around me,
I have lots of dust in the rings,
I am next to Jupiter.

I am the colour of the Earth,
My temperature is 300 degrees,
I have light blue cloud around me.

I am the furthest from the sun,
I am a dark blue planet,
I have a thin ring system.

David Burton (11)
Downham Market High School

What's The Point?

F inding out your middle finger is longest,
L ooking at what someone else is for no reason.
O pening the windows on a cold day,
C atching the soft, furry wisps of air.
C reeping up the stairs when you're home alone.
I ntervals in really short plays at the theatre.
N odding at a question when you mean no.
A uctioning off your favourite items,
U nderstanding the meaning of life.
C ooking a meal you won't eat,
I nventing something that will never work.
N agging at a child when you know it makes no difference.
I mmigrating to a country where you know you aren't welcome.
H eating up a hot classroom by talking.
I nforming someone of something they will never need to know.
L earning subjects that have no point,
I 'll never understand why people become teachers,
P ressurising teenagers with needless exams.
I can't understand the point of golf,
L ooking for a ball in the middle of a forest.
I nterrogating someone you know won't squeal.
F ootballers getting paid loads of money.
I Q tests that mean nothing.
C olouring a picture in black and white.
A ct of estimating as worthless.
T iny Polos when normal Polos are better.
I naccessible items in a shop.
O wning something because your mate does.
N eeding to finish a poem to get to the point.

Well, the point of this poem is *floccinaucinihiliplification*, it's worthless.

Lucy Major (14)
Downham Market High School

Grandad's Garden

They see it every morning
As they walk to get the bus
It can be very nice to see
When the many flowers bloom
But sometimes very sodden
With night or heavy rain
They take their steps with care
Must not spoil or trample
They walk along the stepping stones
To miss the giant mole hills
I like to help them with the harvest
Picking all the runner beans
We dig up the bright red beetroot
And sort the new potatoes
It looks great at evening time
And tea always tastes great
Making it worthwhile
Though it's a muddy job
And it is nearly time
To leave the garden
For the winter wait
It takes up lots of time
But before you know
We can get there again
They hate the weeding though
It seems the same every time
But it tastes the same as well.

Sean Osborn (12)
Downham Market High School

Mr Shadow

Laying over cobbled lanes
Jumping from the walls
Hiding in small crevices
Sleeping in sheltered halls

Dancing around a campfire
Crawling along the trees
Listening to the sound of a lyre
Scaring you with glee

Leaping through the hallways
Flying up the stairs
Sitting on the end of the bed
And confessing to the stuffed bear

Picking on your fear
And moulding it for me
I wait around the corner
And attack like a sting from a bee

Laughing at you all the time
I'm here to let you know
That always I shall be here
And my name is Mr Shadow.

Joshua Walker (14)
Downham Market High School

Teenagers

Why is this,
Girls as teenagers,
Our usual self,
We think of boys, boys and boys,
Boys' bums,
Nice ones,
Big ones,
Small ones,
Take your pick,
Plenty of them,
Some make me sick,
Some have glasses,
Some with freckles,
Nice blue eyes,
Oh yeah, that's nice.
Why is this,
Girls as teenagers,
Our usual self,
We think of town, town and town,
Clothes,
Shoes and make-up,
Cinema,
And being late up,
Claire's, gossip, Geo's,
New Look, labels and HMV,
Girls enjoy most of these,
Maybe you will one day!

Jodie Button (13)
Downham Market High School

Pre-Teen Blues

Coming up to teenage-dom
Thoughts running through my head
Confused about the future
Not sure about the rest

My friends have all betrayed me
I don't know who to trust
They act nice with me, but I can tell
It's 'cause they think they must

My mum's totally against me
My dad agrees with her
My brother's scared when we fight
It's all such a blur

My teachers give me detention
When I've done nothing wrong
My homework takes up all my time
I wish I could have none

People always tease me
Because I like this guy
We're just friends, they can't see that
Even though I try

Coming up to teenage-dom
Don't know how I'll cope
Without someone to help me
I haven't got a hope.

Sophie Drewery (12)
Downham Market High School

The Lover Poem

The smell of smoke fills my room,
Droplets of water fill up my window,
And I think of the place I'd like to be.
I can feel myself in your arms,
I have a smile on my face,
Covered in warmth,
I *never* want to leave this place,
I look at you
And place my hand on your cheek,
And kiss,
Kiss your perfect, soft lips.
Nothing could beat this,
No one could make me feel this loved,
This special.
No words could tell you
How much you mean to me,
This isn't just a fantasy,
I can feel all of this in my heart,
I *never* want us to be apart.

Lewis Hoy
Downham Market High School

The House

Step through the gates like a mouse,
There's the house,
Think it's asleep,
So we might have to creep,
Oh no, it's just leaped,
What was that beep?
Oh, it's a car,
It might take us far,
Come on, let's go,
Jolly ho,
We shall no more creep like a mouse,
Up to that dreadful house.

Tania Arney (12)
Downham Market High School

My Room

My bedroom is a magical place,
Just look around,
Can't you see the smile upon my face?

Dolphins of different colours,
Blue and grey,
Ducking and diving in the sea day after day!

Shelves where I keep my books,
Sounds on my hi-fi,
They're off the hook!

Watching DVDs
And a bed
To catch some Zs.

Having sleepovers,
Eating popcorn and sweets,
What else does a young girl need?

Lorna Collison (11)
Downham Market High School

TV

You turn me on,
You turn me off,
You can't see me in the sun.

Everyone points, it's really rude,
I want to point back,
But I just can't move.

Everyone thinks they are the only one there,
They burp and slurp
And pick their hairs.

I wish I could just walk away,
Day after day,
Here I lay.

Charlotte Hussey (11)
Downham Market High School

Confidential Reality

I'm a silent rebel passing through time barely noticed,
A glimmer a glance, without as much as a speck of a chance,
I stare through frosted glass,
At the images which are broken by censorship
And fear of the forbidden,
Out of these four walls hidden from my reach,
by physical impossibilities
Or the fear of the thrill of the chase,
Expanding day by day at phenomenal pace,
Start the race.
Walls with small doors are everywhere,
But openings are one in a million,
It's only the ones who dare that break out of this small world,
The ones that stand out are a minority,
Influence those that need influencing,
That minority make the majority of minds change,
In the heat of the battle,
They are the ones that keep cool and come out on top,
In pure hope and want for the unknown,
I reach out, arms stretched, for intelligence,
To learn about confidentiality,
The possibility of a different future,
Blending into the crowd isn't a crime but a bore,
The world's presence and the man that stood out is everywhere,
But where is the presence of the man that blends in?
It's nowhere to be seen,
But in the very deepest, darkest depths of that man's soul,
Hiding or not being let out, that's for you to decide,
Where it can't be seen or heard,
Where it can't offend any living being,
A man like this is not a man in my eyes,
No one will remember the name of the boy
That sits silent in the corner,
Hiding himself, from himself,
In my life there are four walls to stop me getting out
And others getting in,

I've pummelled into those walls,
They now lay as piles of dust on the cold, bare floor
That is reality,
Never will I go back into that dark, dank room that is censorship.
There is more out there,
You just have to have the courage,
To go and find it.

Joshua Larner (13)
Downham Market High School

The Key To The World

I am myself, my own person and nobody else,
I wonder what people think of me, do they like me?
Love me? Or hate me?
I hear people talking, laughing, crying,
I see nothing, a blurred vision,
Tears coating my eyes like icing on a cake,
I want to know a way to get out of the world,
No rules, censorship, but where's the key?
I believe that there is a key, a way to freedom,
No censorship, for everyone to be free!
I touch nothing but the cold, hard, frosty air hitting my face,
I worry that no one will ever be able to find the key,
Will they ever be their own person, or will they just go with it?
I dream that somebody finds the key to unlock people from
the crowd,

To make the world free!
Free to live, to express themselves
And not be afraid of who they are!
I feel nothing! Thinking of the future,
Will the key be found before I go or after?
What a mysterious world!

Laura Kenny (13)
Downham Market High School

The Shy, Interactive Whiteboard

Tomorrow is the start of the new term,
Children come to play and learn,
Schools today use technology,
But to me they owe an apology.

In the classes, pupils number 33,
They sit at desks and all stare at me,
They moan and do not want to be there,
I have no choice - life is not fair.

In days of old, teacher used board and chalk,
And to get to school, children had to walk,
But now they use me and my family to learn,
But still for the holiday children yearn.

I dread the days and long for night,
Saturday and Sunday are my delight,
I sit and dread to hear the school bell,
No one knows my fears, I can tell.

I wish and wish sometimes I could be ill,
But always I have to stay here still,
I have heard of a virus which is very bad,
I will catch it soon or surely go mad.

I teach the children, all subjects I take,
But no one asks if I need a break,
No one cares that I am shy,
They don't even know if I cry.

Most of my kind stand tall and proud
And if they could would shout out loud,
I think I make some sort of world record,
I am the one and only shy, interactive whiteboard.

Laura Baker (12)
Downham Market High School

Cat And Dog

I was born into a world
With love all around
The sweet smell of milk
The warmth of my soft quilt

Why was I chosen
To leave all this behind?
The smell of sweet milk gone
No more warmth from my soft quilt

But the cuddles to come
Were the best I've ever known
The world around was warm and kind
Until I met Sam, the Yorkshire terrier

My new, happy home was ripped apart
Chewed at the seams
No more cuddles
No more love

His life was in danger
Of losing what he's got
I helped him home
At the end we shared his bone

Now we are life-long friends
We are cat and dog, Sam and Tiger
We will be together forever
No man or animal can come between us.

Ellen Holden (12)
Downham Market High School

Teddy

I sit and lie on my bed all day
I'm always speechless, nothing to say
The hugs I get are really sweet
I love it when I and my owner meet

I do nothing all day long
I wonder if I've done anything wrong
But I realise that I'm not alone
I and my friends are all at home

It's just that my owner's out
My stitching doesn't let me pout
But when she's here I feel all warm inside
I think, *why was I unhappy, why had I cried?*

I like it when she swings me around
I scream inside, though I make no sound
I like it when we're close together
She hugs me in the stormy weather

I get wet when she cries on my shoulder
But I wasn't wanted as she grew, got older
I think of all the good times we had
To know they're gone, it makes me mad

I wish I could talk and let her know
How I miss and love her so
That one day I tried to talk
My stitching ripped, I was distraught

She never tried to make me right
She never held onto me tight
That day she threw me under the bed
That was the last, nothing else was said.

Kate Hopkin (12)
Downham Market High School

My Life

One day I will be watching TV
And I'll go outside
And be stung by a bee
That's my life

When I am stung by a bee
I'll go back inside
And spill my tea
That's my life

When I spill my tea
I will get up and walk to the beach
And be pushed into the sea
That's my life

So if you ever think of me
This is what will happen
I'll be stung by a bee, spill my tea or get pushed into the sea
That's my life.

Ben Hart (11)
Downham Market High School

Jungle Party

When there's a party in the jungle, everyone comes,
To see the monkeys play the drums.
Tigers playin' the guitar,
Lions at the juice bar.
Toucans popping a balloon,
While giraffes watch the moon.
Everyone is having fun,
Even the moody ones.
At the end of the night,
Everyone has had a bite.
Eating chocolate cake,
Jam tarts and milkshake.
Everyone went home since it was late
And everyone was feeling great.

Katie Williams (12)
Downham Market High School

My Life

My life is like this;
I go to school every week,
But sometimes on a Saturday
I go and watch Norwich City play,
Or I go and play myself for Denver FC.
We are second in our league
And I've scored three goals.
So that's my life today,
But in the future,
I would like to be a footballer.

Thomas English (11)
Downham Market High School

Surf

The curling wave in the day
Smashes onto the sandy bay
Cornish pasty, fish and chips
Locals tell you a few tips.

Going down to the beach
Hire a board, deck chair seat
Walking down with sandy feet
Never know who you'll meet.

In the water, on the board
Never a time to be bored
Catch a wave like a fight
Fast as you can with pure might.

All the fun is so great
This is something no one will hate
It's for old or young
And lots of fun.

Ashton Oakes (11)
Downham Market High School

Bullying

There's bullying all around me,
But that I cannot see.
Teachers tell us not to,
Yet there's nothing they can do.

The big ones always make us wail,
Then we're told, 'No telling tales.'
Others are scared about telling someone,
So the job doesn't get done.

Smack, smack,
Whack, whack,
Hit, hit,
You twit, you twit.

That's what bullies say and do,
To anyone, but no one knows who.

I wish bullying would end,
So this country was on the mend.

So I'm writing this poem today,
To say:
Please make bullying go away!

Becky Bourlet (13)
Downham Market High School

Wedding Day

When that bride walks down that aisle
Upon her face shall be a smile
As we dance to the music's booming sound
Suddenly, glooming all around
She will have the first dance
As graceful as a deer's prance
When they look back on the day
They will see how joyful and gay
In her gown flowing long
As we hear the bells go *ding-dong*.

Daniel Wagg (12)
Downham Market High School

If I Were To Die

If I were to die next week,
Would I be happy? Yes I would.
I've had a chance to live my life
And lived it best I could.

I've loved each day, been with my friends,
Had fun and wondered why.
There's nothing I would change
And I would hope you wouldn't cry.

It would be hard to carry on,
Like I was someone else,
But I hope now you'd be content
And live your life yourself.

If for no one else, just for me
Cos I know I'd be done,
I hope you'd have a wicked one,
I hope that you'd have fun.

Samantha Key (16)
Downham Market High School

How Should I Have You Today?

You can put me up,
You can take me down.
I'm not blinds.

Straighten me!
Curl me!
I love attention.

Don't dye me brown,
I like being blonde.
Don't ruin me!

The wind blows me back,
Put a bow in me!
Clips any colour,
That go with me!

Emily Law (12)
Downham Market High School

Clock Poem

As time goes by
I move round and round
Sometimes I chime
And make a sound

Tick-tock, tick-tock.

Some people may call me 'clock'
But sometimes 'the time'
Lots of people look at me
With my little tick-tock rhyme

Tick-tock, tick-tock.

I'm normally on a wall
Or sitting on a desktop
And way up high
There's normally a big drop

Tick-tock, tick-tock.

Sabrina Barrow (12)
Downham Market High School

Will I Last?

Me mascara
I'm nearly gone
If only she didn't plaster me on
I know she wants to look good
But I do too
Black's not really my colour
That's why I am blue
I make her look fabulous
Yes I do
My writing is fading
So am I
Me in her make-up bag would never last.

Emily Longmuir (12)
Downham Market High School

Poem

She kneels over the dying body,
Her crystal tears drop,
Onto the face of another one
Of death's victims.
Thoughts flash through her mind,
The good,
The bad,
She lays her head,
On her mother's chest
And weeps,
Her mother smiles
Heaves a deep breath,
She's gone,
A scream comes from her open mouth,
The girl brushes away her tears,
Sadness appears over her pale face,
The girl mumbles something,
She looks to the dark sky
And watches as the spirit rises into the sky,
She is suffering no longer.

Amy Grant (12)
Downham Market High School

A House

People come and go,
Some stay for many years,
Or just a month or so.
Different people walked my stairs,
Different people in my rooms,
But me, I'm just the same.

New kitchen,
New rooms,
Old people move out,
New people move in,
But me, I'm just the same.

Alys Williams (12)
Downham Market High School

Best Friends

I've always been there for you,
I've seen all that you've been through,
When you feel sad I feel it too,
I will always love you.

You gave me treats every day
And stayed with me all the way,
You took me out on lots of walks,
I really enjoyed being outdoors.

You took me out to see your friends,
It made me feel safe,
To know how much I meant to you,
To see your happy face.

Now I'm getting older,
It's drawing to an end,
I will always remember you,
My everlasting friend.

Sophie Legge (13)
Downham Market High School

Autumn

The rustling of the leaves
As you walk down a path
That's filled with conkers
And the scent of lovely morning dew.

Hallowe'en trick or treating
The yummy chocolate in our mouths
Feeling quite sick the next morning
But it's so worth it!

Cosying up warm by the fire
And listening to the raindrops
Pitter-patter on the window
I love autumn so much!

Jessica Howling (13)
Downham Market High School

Laughing, Smiling And Giggling

Laughing is something everyone does,
It brightens up the day,
It comes with a smile
And makes me realise what a happy place to be.

People around drinking mugs of coffee,
Having a chat and laughing out loud,
People smile
And make the place a nicer place to be.

Best friends giggling together,
Over marshmallows dipped in chocolate,
Chatting over the latest gossip,
What a great place to be.

Laughing, smiling and giggling,
Help to make the day better for you and me!

Hannah Sanderson (12)
Downham Market High School

Smile

A smile should be big, a smile should be proud,
A smile should be bright, a smile should be loud,
A smile should be given, a smile should be lent,
A smile shouldn't be straightened, a smile shouldn't be bent.

A grin should be happy and full of light,
A grin should be wide and such a pretty sight,
A grin should be copied and made into lots more,
A grin should come from the heart, which is something you
                                            can't ignore.

A laugh should be heard, a laugh should be seen,
A laugh should be echoed, a laugh should be keen.
A laugh shouldn't be quiet, a laugh shouldn't be small,
A laugh should be everything, that's about all.

Zoe Hill (12)
Downham Market High School

I Am Nothing

I live inside an empty house,
I hear, see and do nothing

I'm brown, but fading every day
Cracks up the middle of me
I'm rotting

I don't get slammed, not even shut
Only swaying in the wind throughout the long year

I don't hear the TV playing to itself
I only hear cars go by, it is very rare

I have nothing to do
I will be nothing soon
I will be in a dump
Who knows who I will be with
Or even what I will be?
Do you?

Alex Lawrence (12)
Downham Market High School

My Girl

Someone said she's like beauty incarnate.
Another said she's better with paper
About her head; to them a change of fate
From me - bloody eyes and lost teeth. Later
When I saw her, I held her close to me.
I whispered in her ear softly, 'I love
You.' She smiled at me and kissed so sweetly.
I smiled back, took her hand; like a dove
We went away. I've heard them call us names,
I've seen them point and stare, but we both know
Love has no bounds, so we have no shame.
We're just like another couple on show.
It doesn't matter that you shout and stare;
All that matters is that my one love cares.

Zara-Jade Booth (17)
Downham Market High School

Jealousy

Jealousy is a thing that you hold in forever
Something you can never see
It's a thing that makes you sick inside
Even for you and me.

Hearing people speaking about their lives
Just gives you jealousy
Even hearing people saying
That she looks like someone without money.

Jealousy is something you touch
When you touch another man's suit
Or you're watching the news
On a plasma screen TV.

Jealousy is the taste of blood
When an ulcer pops in your mouth
And the dentist says
He hasn't got any pain relief.

Jedd Desborough (11)
Downham Market High School

The Perfect Man

Before I start I know you don't believe;
Blue eyes, blond hair, white teeth, red lips, bright smile.
It's true! And his body, muscles that heave.
To be with him I will run a whole mile.
He buys me gifts just because he loves me.
When I'm down he listens to my worries.
In fights he is the first to say sorry.
He won't fart or burp after some curries.
What's football? This man loves to go shopping.
Action thriller? He would pick a chick flick.
Housework? A thing of the past - he love mopping.
He'll stay at home and nurse me when I'm sick . . .
Oh! So you've got this far, you do persist,
Don't waste your life and look, they don't exist!

Hayleigh Ilett (17)
Downham Market High School

Anger

Anger is the sound of thunder that crashes
Across the fields and houses,
Like a demon that lashes.

Anger is the smell of fire that blazes
As it licks round the trees in the forest,
Like a million lasers.

Anger is the pain of a rose thorn
As it catches my hand as I touch it,
Like a cat's claw, it scratches.

Anger is the sight of a wave crashing on the seashore
It smashes over the edge of the sea wall,
Like a stallion barging against the stable door.

Anger is the taste of blood trickling from my nose
Then it drips like a splash of red paint,
It stains my clothes.

Emma Symonds (11)
Downham Market High School

The Creature

Once in a deep, dark forest
Lived a formidable creature
With three formidable features,
Who preyed on smaller, less cunning creatures.

Its eyes were as red as fire,
Its mouth only needed one bite to kill.
Nothing could escape it,
But only if they could fight by will.

The less cunning creature only heard snips and snaps,
Then the creature jumped and snapped.
The less cunning creature saw its life
As its bones were being snapped in one big bite.
The creature then walked away
As what was left of the small creature then rotted away.

Robert Brunning (11)
Downham Market High School

To Live In Another Person's Mind

To live in another person's mind
All the thoughts swarming round,
You don't know what you will find
A deep, dark secret may be found.

They could be nasty
They could be kind
They could be feisty
They could be fine.

To live in another person's mind
All the thoughts swarming round,
You don't know what you will find
A deep, dark secret may be found.

They could be sporty
They could be lazy
They could be naughty
They could be crazy.

To live in another person's mind
All the thoughts swarming round,
You don't know what you will find
A deep, dark secret may be found.

Whatever they are
I will not know
I am me
And they are them.

Héloïse Evans (12)
Downham Market High School

Money

I like money
Money buys things
Nice things
Things for me
Things like CDs and games

Money's my friend
It's your friend too
But some people dream for money
Because money buys them things
Nice things
Whatever they want

Some people don't need to dream for money
They've already got it
Money to buy them things
Nice things
They don't care about people who dream for money
People who dream that money would grow on trees
And be their friend

People say money doesn't grow on trees
But it does
It does grow on trees
Trees make paper
Paper makes money
See
I told you
I told you money grows on trees.

Connor Martin (13)
Downham Market High School

Bed

I like to lie on my bed and dream of things to do,
My pillow is soft and squishy,
The quilt is nice and thick too.
So when winter comes I snuggle up tight,
And wonder what I'll dream of tonight,
I've fallen asleep tucked up just right.
When I wake in the morning,
Don't want to get out of bed,
I can't stop yawning,
I'm such a sleepy head.
I wish I could stay in bed all day
And cuddle my big, soft ted
And it's cold outside,
My bed's so warm,
I think I'll stay in here and hide.
Yes, that's what I'm going to do,
Spend the day in my bed,
So Mum says, 'Where are you?'
I say I'm in bed.
'Please let me stay here, Mum!'
'Oh, don't be a sleepy head.'

Rebecca Bettridge (12)
Downham Market High School

Death

Death is such a revolting sight
Whoever sees it will have a horrible fright

Death takes your life away
And you never ever have a say

Death is such a terrible fate
When you are found on the floor by your mate.

Adam Matthews (12)
Downham Market High School

Bonfire Night!

Bonfires crackling, fireworks banging,
Singing and shouting on Bonfire Night.
Catherine wheels spinning,
Everyone's happy on Bonfire Night.
It's a jolly fun time with beer and wine,
We hope you enjoyed it on *Bonfire Night!*

Ally Bailey (11)
Downham Market High School

Happiness

Happiness is my cat curled up on my knees
My dog curled up at the end of my bed
I stroke their fur contentedly
I cuddle my teddies

Happiness is my favourite music in my ears
The rustle of money that I hear
The laughter of people having fun
Bees making new honey

Happiness is the smell of a cake
Cooking on a winter's day
Fresh out of the oven
While the children go out to play

Happiness feels like really soft teddies
When I'm scared at night
Feeling all snuggly and warm
Holding them really tight

Happiness is a big bar of Galaxy
Creamy and chocolatey and sweet
Lovely taste on my tongue
Makes me feel complete.

Charlotte Gingell (11)
Downham Market High School

Love Poem

Love is a big, bubbly bath
Which I soak in day and night
It keeps me relaxed every night
And it keeps me very light.

Love is the sound of relaxing music
On a miserable, rainy day
It's calm and soothing listening to music
Which calms my troubles away.

Love is a sweet scent of a summer's day
In a field with roses and lavender
The sun shines down on the colourful buds
And the smell that lasts all day.

Love is cuddling a soft ball, dog, puppy
Leaning back into a soft, scented bed
Squeezing your favourite teddy
Lifting a newborn baby above.

Love is a giant bar of melted chocolate
Which you can dip your strawberry in
I bring my strawberry to your lips
Then you kissed my lips.

Amy Bilton (12)
Downham Market High School

Random Weather

Blue sky, green grass
How original
I like winter
Winter is white

White winters
Snowy cold
Ooh, ice
Icy blasts

Wet and cold
Dull and icy
Sun's all gone
No sun

Umbrellas, umbrellas
It's rainy weather
They have
Shape and style

Oh, the weather
The sunny weather
Is back
And the snow is gone.

Francesca Pilcher (13)
Downham Market High School

Animals

Animals, animals, animals!
That's all I ever think about.
Lions, snakes, crocodiles, birds, lizards,
They all seem to amaze me.

The lion is fierce
And frightening face to face.
It is a bit scary,
But really it's a lovely creature.

Snakes are cold,
I have one at home.
Slippery, wriggly, jiggly to hold,
But bite you if you harm them.

Birds, the flying animal,
The beak, the wings, the feet,
All the amazing features,
But I love the deadly, frightening eye of the eagle.

Crocs, the water creature,
Hard skin and it's rock hard.
Sharp teeth that can crack a skull,
Only if you harm it.

Lizards, my fave of all animals,
The way they move, the way they live
And all the other cool ways,
Not very deadly, but can still leave a nasty bite.

Well, I have come to an end,
Animals are great, I have to go now,
So don't kill animals, they are just like me and you,
I must go,
Animals, animals, animals!

Joseph Shade (13)
Downham Market High School

Metal On Flesh

He came into my life, so young, energetic, dynamic,
Now I do not understand why it happened, I cannot grasp the reality.
I hear it now, the scream of the banshee as it closes in,
Each second is eternity as the racing monster draws nearer
                                                    and nearer,
I can feel the fear, taste the death, the cruel destruction of life.
So young, fresh, full of life, unjustly taken.
Eight inches separated life from death, happiness from pain,
Even now I can taste the burning of rubber,
Metal on flesh, metal on flesh, flesh on metal, metal on flesh.
His little body mangled, his face unrecognisable.
The image imprinted forever on my brain -
Why must I forever lose those around me?
Why must it be I who is the one to suffer?
An action like a flicker, a bat of an eyelid, imposes years of pain.
I see the trail of love he left behind, shattered and destroyed,
Why had they not realised what they had done?
The anger swells within me, looking at the consequences, the lack
                                                    of care,
Metal on flesh, metal on flesh, flesh on metal, metal on flesh.
I gaze into the sky and scream a torrent of rage,
The innocent punished by the guilty, the pure blemished by
                                                    the tainted.
If only they had known, would care have been exercised?
Metal on flesh, metal on flesh, flesh on metal, metal on flesh.

Jimmy Watkinson (17)
Downham Market High School

Why?

Why do people die and make us cry?

Why can't they stay with us forever
Instead of leaving us heartbroken, with a gap in our lives?

Do they know what's happening
When they shut their eyes for the last time?

Are they still thinking as you hope they would be,
Or is their brain just dead?

I hate it when people say that word - dead,
What a horrible word!

Do you know where you are
Or do you just sleep forever?

Heaven? Is it real? Do the angels look after you
Or are you just left helpless? I hope not!

Why is it that you lose the special people,
The good people, not the horrible and nasty people?

Why can't dreams and wishes come true?
Why can't you bring them back?

Why?

Sophie Davis (13)
Downham Market High School

I Can't Write A Poem

I can't write a poem,
Words just fail me.

I try and try,
But I still stare into space.

I've got poetic block all the time,
But I've just written a poem!

George Godfrey (11)
Downham Market High School

Hallowe'en

My favourite holiday, Hallowe'en
Scary and gruesome, masks and costumes come to life
Trick or treaters come to your door, asking for sweets and candy.

Wolves howl at the moon
Brittle winds whip through their coats
Pumpkins glow out of windows, lighting up the dark streets.

Witching hour, ghouls and ghosts come to life
Walking or floating through the graveyard
Corpses tear away the soil to see the full moon.

Sophie Cotgrove (13)
Downham Market High School

Holidays

Why is it people go on holidays
Buy big balloons
Or maybe ice cream?
What about strawberry?

Sun, sand, sea
That's the life for me
Buckets, spades and shells
Sandcastles standing tall.

People running on the sand
Collecting really big shells
Brightly coloured kites
Flying through the night.

This is why people go on holiday
To have a lot of fun
And eat a lot of ice cream
Maybe even strawberry.

Emily Griffiths (14)
Downham Market High School

The Serpent

The ancient Norsemen named him Jörmungandr,
In the Bible he is Leviathan, destroyer of Atlantis,
Those who know of the Arcane ways call him Ouroboros,
We will never know his true name, as this word only came
                                    from the mouths of the fallen,
But he is one thing, the great serpent,
Architect of the Apocalypse.

Look around you.
See the crumbling buildings, cracked pavements, and you
                                    can see him.
His mighty head looms over our cities, his eyes blaze like the
                                    eternal flames of Hell,
His colossal body carving invisible trenches in our land.
That same fire burns inside us all,
You can see it in the eyes of the hooded thugs that linger
                                    in the alleyways,
Deciding who may have something worth taking from them,
The bank teller sees his wicked stare down the barrel of the gun
                                    shoved into her face,
As the desperate man screams for the money.

Under Earth he lies and under steel, under stone he lies
                                    and under sea,
A frozen abyss where no human thought has dared venture,
Fed by malice and man's inhumanity to Man, he feels the time of
                                    reckoning draw near,
Continents will be torn asunder and dragged into the deep,
The heavens shall weep with his flaming breath.

He forms in the fumes of the car that cuts your path,
The ogre at the wheel, fraught with road rage, ensnared in his tasks
                                    that are far more important than pedestrians,
Not giving thought to how close he came to knocking you down.
Even if he had, he probably wouldn't have stopped.

Tremors shake the ground as two armies approach each other,
Tyrannical powers pushing them ever forward,
A soldier sees the face of the man that he will kill.
Bombs are detonated, deadly light swelling in spheres.
Blood is spilt.
Can you feel that?
The serpent stirs.

Henry Agger (16)
Downham Market High School

My Friend

We'll be friends forever
I just know it
Through thick and thin
I'll be there
And I know you'll be there too

We argue and fight
But I never mean it
And nor do you
We always make up

You always put a smile on my face
You're my best friend
And without you
I'm just me

The tears
And laughs
The late night calls
And the secrets shared

I'll be there for you
Till the day I die
You're the best friend a girl could have
So I just want to say *thanks!*

Holly Owen (13)
Downham Market High School

The Rose

(In memory of September 11th, 2001)

A rose in a fisted glove,
A shocking symbol; like a slaughtered dove,
It's funny really, 'cause I hate birds!
Pictures, visions, worth a thousand words.

The smell of a rose; aromatic, perfume,
Purity? Yes. Innocence? Yes. Love? No.
Among men, easily said that it exists,
Watch the television, read the newspapers. All torn to bits.

The petal juice runs through their fingers.
Thick, red, valuable. God's presence lingers
Forever. His prized possessions, works of art,
Spilled on dirt, grass. Broken into two; hearts.

The stalk is the hardest to crush it seems,
Makes a rose, a rose. Ignored with ease.
And I wonder if a rose feels the burn down there, like us,
When they're mercilessly picked off without a care, like us.

And so the rose is torn by the fisted glove.
A shocking symbol; like a slaughtered dove.
And so we're in the hands of each other,
One lives, whilst the other dies.
Think of the child with no television, no newspapers,
But who can feel that burn

As he cries.

Gemma Hambright (16)
Downham Market High School

I Love Shopping

Girls love shopping
Girls love clothes
Girls love gossip
Girls love shoes
But it all costs money!

Shopping for birthdays
Shopping for parties
Shopping for Christmas
Shopping for fun
But it all costs money!

Going into New Look
Going into Tammy
Going into MKOne
Going into River Island
But it all costs money!

Having a bite to eat
Having a McDonald's
Having fun with mates
Having a good old gossip
But it all costs money!

Getting very excited
Getting very tired
Getting very moody
Getting to the end of the day
But it all costs money!

Ana Boughen (13)
Downham Market High School

Vampire

I'm a misfit of the world
I only come out at night
I sleep during the day inside a coffin
I drink the blood of the humans to quench my thirst.

After that, they are dead, but still alive
They become my slaves
A zombie that cannot think.

They are hunting me now . . .
The humans of the world
I can't escape
I start to sprint
But it's no use, the sun is rising.

The light is bright, I feel my skin burning
I start to scream and yell as the sun gets brighter
I'm on my knees in pain
Soon I will be gone
I start to bubble and burn inside . . .
Until I'm nothing but dust.

Thomas Sheppard (13)
Downham Market High School

You're A Loser

You're a loser
And you're a snoozer
You play football bad
You smell like Mikey
And you're mad.

You are lazy
And you make everyone crazy
You snap and you slap.

So you're a loser
And you play like a loser
So *ha, ha, ha!*

Sam Howard (12)
Downham Market High School

TV

TV, loads of things in a box
Casualty, too much blood, ugh
Can't stand it, even chickenpox
When it ends, phew!

But the TV guide, weird
The crossword, wrong answer, scribble
A man with a beard
The picture in the middle.

Racing, fast, fast cars
People hit, *bang, wallop*, typical
They get hit so, so far
Then they go to hospital.

Volume goes up so, so loud
Earplugs, need earplugs
Sounds like a large crowd
Feels like my eardrums are being tugged.

I go for the off button
Nearly there, got to get there
But I feel like I'm walking to Saturn
Got it off, now I can relax in my chair.

Lewis Bond (13)
Downham Market High School

Arsenal

A rsene Wenger is the one who orders them about
R eyes running up the line
S enderos holding the back four
E boue running up and down
N utmegging other teams
A rsene running rings and rings
L eading the Champions League with 20 points, *yippee!*

Peter Howling (11)
Downham Market High School

'What The . . .' I Said!

I lay at night,
I think what might happen next,
I think I might
Go back to sleep.

I heard, *knock, knock,*
There was a creature at the door.
He said, 'Hot sock.'
'What the . . .' I said.

'Hot sock,' he said.
He had a funny little hat.
'Hot sock,' he said.
'What the . . .' I said.

He wore a suit,
With a funny little red tie.
He said, 'You're cute.'
'What the . . .' I said.

'Hot sock,' he said.
I looked at his socks and I saw
Some red-hot flames.
'What the . . .' I said.

It was my dad's foot on fire.
Oh no!

Beth Kidd (11)
Downham Market High School

Happiness

Happiness is a puppy, golden-brown
It is a lovely chocolate melted alone
And it is waiting to sit down by my side
When I am doing my work at home

Happiness is love like a fluffy pillow
It is stroking the trunk of a willow
The smell of rose and lavender
It is the touch of the fluffy petals

Happiness is a thing that cannot be named
But it is a homework not explained
It is someone who was late
And has to work on a piece of slate

Happiness is a puppy, golden-brown
It is the frown of someone you hate
It is the love of your family or your mate
It's happiness.

Shannon Gibbs (11)
Downham Market High School

Friends

F unny, happy, jokey people
R unning, walking, talking people
I ce cream, chips and picnic people
E njoying life and weekends people
N ever lying, truthful people
D efending you and others people
S elfish no, caring yes, these are my favourite people.

Eloise Braun (14)
Downham Market High School

Plank

I am a plank,
A plank of wood,
I used to be a tree
And I was born when they cut down
The former version of me.

I am a plank,
I sit in a boat
And sail the seven seas,
Looking for an island,
With rocks, a beach and trees.

I am a plank,
I lie on the roof,
Of one of their tiny abodes
And I do my best to keep out,
The wind, the rain and snows.

I am a plank,
In tatters and shreds,
Attacked by rebellious troops,
The villagers they were rounded up
And led away in groups.

I am a plank,
In a small bundle,
Wrapped up in thick, sodden rope,
I get taken to a settlement,
They'll be nice to me, I hope.

I am a plank,
On a wood fire,
I should have run and fled,
Goodbye my good companion,
For now, I am dead.

Galen Reich (12)
Downham Market High School

Ned The Bed-Head

There's a boy with the name of Owen,
Who likes to see things glowing,
He's never out of bed, so kiss his head,
Sweet dreams for Owen.

He always wants pizza,
But he also loves liver,
He thinks he is the best,
So don't get in a mess,
He will never say yes.

His favourite toys are his foxes,
He keeps them in his boxes,
So listen to what he says,
He's there every other day.

Owen's hair is always messy,
The same as him being stressy,
He always wants to gel his hair,
But his mum says he has to sit on the special chairs.

Owen learning about all the fun he can have,
If he gets out of bed,
It's his birthday.

Rhys Rose (11)
Downham Market High School

Raven

Raven is a cat killing a mouse
Which bothers me all night
It keeps me at risk and threatens me to die
And it stops me from doing everything right
Raven is the sound of a person shouting
On a rainy day
That noise that freaks you out
A raven squeezing its prey
Raven is the smell of a pair of gym socks
That smell so vile
Trapped in a locker
Which reeks for more than a mile
Raven is horrid, like touching a rat's remains
Leaning back to spikes so spiky
Squeezing a snail
As you would say in Australia, crikey
Raven is eating puke from an 80-year-old
Sucking through a mouldy straw
Keep sucking more and more
Like snogging a boar.

Owen Mills (11)
Downham Market High School

Anger Poem

Sight is what Hell brings down
You never know what will come
You're always seeing things, except when you are asleep at home
You never know what you will see next
You can hear Hell below, it's the sound you don't want to hear
It's always there, blinding bright
But it is a bad sight
That you can't fight
Anger you can smell, it smells like something burning
Burning red-hot
Red-hot and fiery
Burning red-hot and lightning-bright
Anger you can touch
It feels all rough and bumpy
Like a pile of stones you put your hand over
When you put your hand over, it feels like you're touching Hell
Anger tastes like red-hot peppers you swallowed whole
The burn never goes
Your mouth is always on fire
Even if you drink two litres of water, the burn won't go away.

Robert Self (11)
Downham Market High School

Smiles

Smiles
You can see a smile from miles
Some things can't smile, like tiles
Some places there are no smiles
Like trials.

They're the best things in the world are smiles
Some people keep smiles in piles
And don't forget in files
I know lots of people with smiles
Lots of them go for miles.

Some smiles stretch for miles
Others are no bigger than small tiles
But they're all still smiles.

Smiles
You can see a smile from miles
Some places have no smiles
Like trials.

Joseph Rolph (12)
Downham Market High School

Justice

Good is something kind and caring,
Evil is mean, nasty and daring.
A scream is heard by a lady's shout,
'Please give it back,' but no one's about.
The man runs off with the lady's bag,
For all he knows she'll be left in rags.
But he is bad, so he doesn't care,
His life is probably dull and bare.
He gets his kicks out of people's pain,
That's the way he gets his gain.

Good is something kind and caring,
Evil is mean, nasty and daring.
Guns are blazing, the trigger is pulled,
Bang, bang, bang! the police are called.
A getaway car is waiting outside,
They all jump in, here goes their ride.
The police are hot on their tracks,
They'd better go fast and watch their backs.
An hour has passed and they drive so fast,
A skid, a screech, they fall short,
Game over, handcuffed and finally caught.

Stephanie Siegert (11)
Downham Market High School

Despair

The darkness floods in
Like an overflowing river
The coldness seeps in
And sends a cold shiver

Down the spine of the captured
With clothes ragged and worn
Covered in mud
And stretched and torn

Chained to a wall
With no chance of escape
No way to cry out
With their mouths covered in tape

Only stale bread and water
For breakfast and tea
And maybe some cheese
If they were extremely lucky

They all tried to escape
But got caught one day
They were sentenced to death
And locked far away

Now just for you people
Who think life is fun
Take time to reflect
On every one

Not everyone has the life you lead
Fresh food and clean water
There are others in need!

Tamara Horscroft (11)
Downham Market High School

Love You

I think our love is gentle
Burning warm and bright

I am always there for you
We know that this is right

You understand the pain I'm in
You're always by my side

I will always love you
This I cannot hide

We share our love together
Through all the good and bad

Together we are grateful
For all that we have had

Hopeful we will stay this way
Forever and a day

A love like this will never end
For this we both will pray.

Catherine Farnham (11)
Downham Market High School

The Crazy Scientist

There is a crazy scientist in our town,
His name is Bob and he looks like a clown.
He creates things, we would not like to say,
Come with me, let's check out his day!

It's alive, it's alive! Oh no, not that!
It's his protégé, Frankenstein, but he's terribly fat.
He thumps and bumps around the floors,
Bashing and crashing and smashing into doors!

It works! It works! What? No, not that!
A twirly, whirly aeroplane hat.
It twists and turns his crazy head,
Making him dizzy so he collapses on his bed.

There is a crazy scientist in our town,
His name is Bob and he often wears a large frown.
So beware, take care whenever you are out,
Because crazy Bob's inventions can make you shout!

Sophie Alexander (11)
Downham Market High School

All Hallows Eve

While children are getting ready for trick or treating,
The supernatural gather for their annual meeting.

Visiting every house in sight,
Collecting goodies till late at night.

With mouths full of toffee, marshmallows and sweets,
Giggles and laughter ring out on the streets.

But down in the graveyard the restless awaken,
The ghostly revisit the world they've forsaken.

By midnight the children will be tucked up in bed
And ghosts will return to the land of the dead.

Eleanor Smith (11)
Downham Market High School

Poem

There's armies of people to write about
But how?
There's animals, flowers and people,
All to be written about.
What about me and you?
We should be written about.
Doctors and police and families too,
Tigger, Tweety and Pooh.
There's just another few,
Authors, poets and singers
To be considered too.
Heroes, heroines and devils,
All in the name of the Lord,
Settlements, wars and lots more,
Too many things don't you think?

Rebecca Barwick (11)
Downham Market High School

Changing Wizards

Is a wizard good or evil?
If he changed a man to a lad,
If he changed a forest to wood
Would you say that he is bad
Or would you say that he is good?
When you decide, remember this,
He's on your side,
(I wrote this as a little twist).

Megan Wilkinson (11)
Downham Market High School

For My Birthday I Would Like

For my birthday I would like:
A day, just Mum and me,
Doing whatever we wish,
To go on a shopping spree
Would be great,
Or maybe relax all day.

For my birthday I would like:
A trip around the world,
To China, Berlin or France.
I'd buy everything there,
All day long.
It's not much I want, of course.

Elizabeth Young (12)
Downham Market High School

Hypnotism

Blankly talking,
Lifelessly walking,
Take a second glance,
You're under a trance.

You're under their power,
Do their bidding for hours,
Bow down to your king,
Then forget everything.

Blankly talking,
Lifelessly walking,
Have no feelings or thoughts,
More a chance you'll get caught.

You're under their power,
Do their bidding for hours,
You're under a spell,
That will send you to Hell!

Amy Rayner (12)
Downham Market High School

Is The Demon Headmaster A Hypnotist?

Is the demon headmaster a hypnotist?
I cannot really say,
But I wish he'd go away!

Is the demon headmaster a hypnotist?
He won't show,
It's making me feel low!

Is the demon headmaster a hypnotist?
I really want to get it out,
I don't have any doubt!

Is the demon headmaster a hypnotist?
I have cracked it, it's really true!
Watch out, he might just hypnotise you!

Emma Appleby (11)
Downham Market High School

Good Vs Evil

The Devil's eyes fell upon the room
Of good and the evil mood began to loom.
The green-eyed monster entered the crowd,
The Devil's presence was clear and loud.
The angel returned,
The Devil was burned.
The angel ruled,
So the jealousy cooled.
But sooner or later,
The evil is greater.
With emerald eyes, green as gems,
The monster's evil starts to stem.
Beware, beware, don't get caught up,
Stay good, stay good, for the angel is up.
The evil is gone,
So good rules on.
The angel rises,
The good receive prizes.

McKayla Pickwell (11)
Downham Market High School

Victim Of His Hypnotism

The stone on the pendulum swung from left to right,
A glittering, glimmering little ball of light,
He took off his glasses and let me see
A power so strong I was unable to flee.
For a minute I could swear his eyes flashed red,
Balls of fire set into his head.
Then they began to devour my soul,
My mind was spinning into a black hole.

A crashing alerted me an hour later,
I was lying inside a meteor crater . . .
'This is an illusion,' I heard an echoing voice say,
'When you wake up, you will forget the whole day.'
With eyes now green as a stormy sea,
Flooding my lungs, drowning me,
His voice had a very metallic tone,
Whining somehow, starting to groan.

Against my will, I started to walk
To a sketch of a building, on the floor in chalk.
Could I hear someone talking about a bank?
My mind had gone completely blank.

I wandered home, pondering why
I spent the whole day looking at the sky.
As I reached home, a policeman was there,
My mother looked shocked, sitting silently on a chair.
'Mum?' I called, in disbelief,
What could have caused her this grief?
'Five million pounds!' she suddenly gasped,
Then she realised I was in a trance . . .

Florence Mather (11)
Downham Market High School

If I Could Make A Whole New World

If I could make a whole new world,
I would cancel out history and maths,
I would make sure that all the boys in the world
Would have to have regular baths.
I'd make sure that I could be very rich
And poor people wouldn't exist.
In my new world I would also make
Hunger a long-lost myth.
Yes, I'd make sure we only need to eat
To please our bored little minds,
We wouldn't need to drink either
And everyone would be kind.
Another thing I'd get rid of
Would be spiders, huge and hairy,
I'd replace them with silver diamonds
Because diamonds aren't as scary.
One more thing I'd love to have
Is snow, guaranteed in December.
To have it on Christmas Day would be great,
Then it would be one to remember!
Finally, I know, I would make
Much longer holidays,
For, in my opinion, we work too hard,
We should work far shorter days!

Chloe Woolmer (12)
Downham Market High School

The Endless Journey

As the glazing moonlight swoops down onto the subtle sand,
The metallic sea rode in and out of the never-ending harbour.
The tender whistle of the thriving wind,
Hollows along the bleak skies,
Morphing through anything in its path.
The footsteps of a gentle nothing,
Crosses the plain of sand,
Disturbing only the wind's powerful journey across the seas.
Hush! The wind becomes a gentle breeze, the ocean still.
Nothing. Could this be the end of an endless journey?
Daylight!

Jazzmine Barrett (11)
Downham Market High School

Cars

Cars are red, cars are blue,
We all know cars are brill,
They're fast, they're slow,
But still,
The Reliants, they're cracky,
Toppling over more than a drunk driver.

I'm a pink large Chevy V8,
Speeding along the roads,
When I get out, people clap and cheer,
When they see me coming.

People come and laugh,
But soon as they arrive,
They go away fast,
If only I could have a speedy friend,
Or even a long drive.

If only, if only I could have all these things,
Cos they seem so good . . .

Oliver Skeels (11)
Downham Market High School

The War On Downham Market

Up in Downham Market
A war is breaking out
The good guys and the bad guys
Begin to scream and shout.

The tanks are lining up outside
The library and the school
They're bombing all the bridges
The classrooms and the hall.

They turn their attention to the clock
Standing proud and tall
But with ten shots of a Challenger
It stands there no more.

Soon the Navy is involved
And they sail down the Ouse
Sadly they run aground and can't
Save the town hall.

The airforce are on their way
And fly across the school
But they make a dodgy shot
And the E Block, it does fall.

Out come the teachers
With machine guns and grenades
They are the ones who stop it
Like terrorists on parade.

The only bad thing is
We have to go to school again.

Patrick Bishop (11)
Downham Market High School

Me

I live in a house, opposite the green,
Right next to the pub, it's easily seen.

My ten-year-old sister is Milly,
She's OK, but sometimes rather silly.

We have a dog each, so that's fine,
I love Harry best cos he's mine.

I breed guinea pigs out in the shed,
It's my job to make sure that they're fed.

My hobbies include horse riding,
Seeing my friends and dancing.

With homework as well, I'm quite busy,
And now I've got a kitten called Dizzy.

Beth Pike (11)
Downham Market High School

Hypnotism

My eyes are slowly closing,
Falling into a trap,
Can't remember what is happening,
Nothing is in focus anymore.

Obeying every rule that's set,
Following the head in charge,
What is going on?
Deep, deep, deep asleep.

Slowly coming back now,
Eyes gradually opening,
Everything is a blur,
My head is aching.

Back in focus now,
The past forgotten,
Standing up to leave the room,
What happened? Will I ever know?

Elizabeth Bates (11)
Downham Market High School

My Friend

What a lovely way to end the day,
By sitting in the sun when you're driving home
Cos you have finished work
And you say, 'I'm almost done.'
You walk into your house as quiet as a mouse
And you think, yes you think that you've heard
And outside on a branch of a tree,
Is a very small bluebird.
'Why, hello my little friend,'
You quietly say to this small thing,
And when you look, it appears to have an injured wing,
So you take it into the house to repair its damaged arm
And as you do so, you find out it hasn't done much harm.
So you place it back on the branch of your garden tree
And as you do so, you say,
'Bye-bye, you were a lovely friend to meet.'

Cara Rose (11)
Downham Market High School

The Demon Headmaster

The,
The demon,
The demon headmaster,
Hypnotising everyone,
Every one of the goodie-goodies,
The normals never take a chance,
If you were to see him you would definitely say,
'Oh my word, what a strange man.'
He is very weird,
Oh my word, his glasses,
What a strange man.
We had a plan,
To see what he really says,
But of course it didn't work,
What a strange man.

Jessica Russell (11)
Downham Market High School

All Sports

Chaos on the football pitch,
As Adam misses a tackle,
Chaos on the football pitch,
As Alex heads home,
Chaos on the football pitch,
As Patrick hits the bar,
Chaos on the football pitch,
As Peter scores an own goal.

Chaos on the cricket pitch,
As Jack bowls the batsman out.
Chaos on the cricket pitch,
As two fielders collide.
Chaos on the cricket pitch,
As the batsman hits a six.
Chaos on the cricket pitch,
As the fielder makes a catch.

Chaos on the tennis court,
As Tom does a bad serve.
Chaos on the tennis court,
As David wins the set.
Chaos on the tennis court,
As Tom wins David's serve.
Chaos on the tennis court,
As Tom wins the match.

Sam Sharp (12)
Downham Market High School

The Mistake

The night passes slowly,
It's almost unbearable,
The house is silent, not a sound in the air,
I don't think anyone dares to care.

I can't bear it any longer,
I haul myself up from my soft, miserable bed of rest.

As I walk past the bathroom,
I hear the only sound that I've heard in a long time;
The lonely, sorrowful tap trying to gain attention.
I grant its wish and turn it off, to let it rest in peace.

A sound comes from downstairs,
Do I dare go down?
Something's wrong, I can feel it in my bones,
What have I done? I thought it was right,
I only meant to give her a fright.

As I go downstairs, I see her there,
Sitting still, looking cold,
What have I done? Will she ever like me again?
Will she ever forgive me?

Ellen Atkinson (11)
Downham Market High School

Love

Love is the duvet that I cuddle at night
Which holds me in my bed so tight at night
Love is sweet as an apple.

Love is all about the laughter
On a hot day in the summer
And hearing the birds sing a lovely tune.

Love is a beautiful scent of an autumn day
Love is the smell of freshly cut grass
The smell that lasts all day.

Love is stroking the fur of a young kitten
Leaning back into big teddies
Lifting a newborn kitten high above.

Love is watching a soppy film
And eating a big, big bar of chocolate
With your newborn kitten.

Zoey Bates (11)
Downham Market High School

Taken Away

As I wait for him
Sitting, waiting
Wanting to see him one last time
Wishing, wanting
Have they already taken him?
Selfish, white
All because of his colour, culture
Different, black
A perfect man
Cheap slave
Now shipped away
Never to return
I want him back
Freedom.

Eve Tilsley (15)
Framingham Earl High School

Views

I know me
And I am happy as I am,
But I try to see through others' eyes,
Get their point of view.

I try to see through a friend's eyes,
Try to understand her,
See how she cares about what other people think,
Try not to embarrass her.

I try to see through a friend's eyes,
Try to understand her,
Relish in her carefree attitude,
Love being her.

I try to see through a friend's eyes,
Try to understand her,
Feel the pain, the suffering,
Try to make her better.

I try to see through others' eyes,
But ultimately I'm me,
I'll never see the same as them,
But I do try.

Jessie Taylor (13)
Framingham Earl High School

She Didn't Want This

A baby lies patiently in the nurse's arms,
Her doe-eyed face sparkling with tears.
Saltwater streaking her tiny cheeks,
Her hands thrashing out of her pink blanket.
The social worker stands, creating a shadow over them.
The baby, slowly passed to the social worker.
The baby cries out helplessly for her mother.
She didn't want this to happen.

Verity Roat (12)
Framingham Earl High School

United By Passion

United.
Together once again,
The voice of our leader,
Repairing our wounds, broken hearts and souls,
United.
With our passion aflame,
Smelling like the devotion,
Of a mother to her child,
And the taste,
The juice of the sweetest mango,
A drop, my taste buds are alive,
United.
The uproar of the joyful cries,
Hiding the raw pain and suffering,
Fill the world with warmth,
As they watch,
The flames of the fire,
And its burnt out remains.
United.
Passion leads us forwards,
Passion makes us fight,
Passion beats our hearts,
Passion is all we need to win,
Our journey to total racial equality.

Florence Auckland (13)
Framingham Earl High School

Love

I turned over once,
To look at my loved one,
But there she didn't lie.

I blinked once,
Thought I was dreaming,
But realised I was far away.

I could hear her voice,
I could smell her perfume,
But still she wasn't near.

Shivers ran through my spine,
Her hands pressed mine,
I turned, to realise I was dreaming.

Layla Howe (15)
Framingham Earl High School

Peace

Peace is a river,
Sweeping across the land,
Swilling out all the evil,
Washing the world of its sins.

Gaining more followers as it goes,
Feeding people; upholding life.
The river spreads its love and happiness,
Giving people hope and faith.

Sometimes the river may slow down
But not for long
There will always be
A place of peace, somewhere.

Charlotte Long (13)
Gresham's Senior School

Just Like The Night We Left

Gravel skips away from my feet
Dancing in the silver night
Reflecting central orbs of light
Hanging in the skies

Halogen coins spill out the door
Drawing us up
Then upstairs to candlelit dinners
The ebb and flow of quiet conversation
Mingled with the waves below

I rush to the telescope
Eight years old again
To peer down its narrow shaft
Just like the night we left

Ferry glides on rippling glass
Breaking light within its path
Buoys bobbing on diamond sea
Bunting fussing in the breeze
Ice cream sign waving proudly
Just like the night we left

Standing eight years high
On the platform a voice calls
I back away
Knowledge of leaving heavy in my mind
Yet a smile lifts my mouth
As I catch my reflection

The same black smoky O
Rings my eye
Panda-like I turn laughing
Back to my family
Just like the night we left.

Clemmie van Hasselt (14)
Gresham's Senior School

Sacred Heart

Striding down the familiar drive,
The welcoming, warning statue of Mary greets me.
The gravel crunches under my little girl lace-ups,
Feeling lost, longing and six years old.

My adolescent frame clumsily runs through the shrunken playground,
Chased by the crisp breeze as it slaps at my child's cheeks.
I gasp for air, tie tied tight as any chains.
Hopscotch, skipping, train ride.
I glide through the memory, dreading the bell.

9.15
Silently slipping past the chapel, the sound of an organ playing,
Seeps through the door,
I can no longer run and shout and play,
But I must pray . . . amongst the many shuffling nuns from foreign
destinations.

Secretly, I long for a smooth, round, hard conker to run through my
fingers,
Gazing through the pink, yellow, blue stained glass my mind wonders.
Hanging pristinely above the sisters' garden,
Habit after habit after habit . . .
And a giggle escapes from my lips.

I feels so real, so right, so wrong.
To this Catholic world I no longer belong,
For me the Sacred Heart is gone.

Tash Milne (14)
Gresham's Senior School

Limbo

The light to life
Silently snaps shut behind them
Sealing their fate.

Herded by harpies,
Like battered bodies,
Prisoners of war
In this concentration camp.

Bright white of marbled eyes
Stare with menace
From the shadows.

Their choral shrieks
Bruised as they echo
Off the walls.

Nostrils flared in fear,
Evacuating
The vile stench
Which lines their lungs.

Each waiting their turn.

Quivering bodies
Career
Around the small sphere
They inhabit.

Singled out
By the metal arm of God,
Cold steel
Pressed against the warm
And now clammy flesh

The large beast trembles,
Aftershock.

Isobelle Miller (17)
Gresham's Senior School

. . . Wake Up To Blue . . .

Wake up

the voices whisper
their soft song of the sea
on the hull
sloshing steady slapping
rhythmic lapping

The high *chink chink*
of masts up above
The slatting of a sandal
on asphalt

The world around busy
already busy

As deep as the sea of sky
was my slumber but
as engines started
the sea mist
in my head

Clearing   Clearing

The Ionian Sea
No rules no laws
Happily at peace
Gwynt-y-Mor.

Kimberley Bennett-Abbiss (14)
Gresham's Senior School

The Race

The adrenaline is pumping through me,
A hill ahead looks ever so steep,
The start line is all I can see,
I can imagine the rewards I hope to reap.

We're off!

My breath is rasping in my throat,
The wind is whistling in our hair,
The speed makes me feel afloat,
To win the race is my only care.

We hit the slope, we puff and blow,
The pain is lancing through our thighs,
And still we both refuse to slow,
Anticipating the victor's prize.

We're up and on the downward slope,
I know my swift opponent is on my tail,
All I can do is pedal and hope,
Why is it I'm as slow as a snail?

And now he's up with me, up by my side,
I think, *oh no, we're going to crash*,
We cross the line and end this ride,
By skidding and only now I see the lake, *splash!*

Henry Blower (14)
Gresham's Senior School

The Game

You get off the bus, fresh and raring to go,
You stretch off all your stiff and tense muscles,
You get the ball moving in a consistent flow,
The ref checks your studs and meets the captains,
You take off your tracksuits and get ready to put on a show.

The huddle is formed and you chant your team name,
When the starting whistle is blown,
You hope your team won't be put to shame,
The first hard hit is made and a try scored,
Before you know It, it's the end of the game.

The tunnel is formed at the end of the match,
With the shake of a hand you leave the field,
Bruised and cut from a sharp stud scratch,
Exhausted and tired as you reach for the nearest drink,
Followed by a brief talk from the coach about the match.

Will Scott (13)
Gresham's Senior School

Light

Is light something
That just enables you to see?

Does light just mean it isn't heavy?
Is it another word
Trying to describe 'low fat'
No weight, not heavy?

Or perhaps just a name for a softer colour,
A softer blue, a paler red?

Isn't light a symbol or representative
For an opportunity which has re-opened
Or another chance
A new road?

Light, an over-used word?
Or is it more?

Sophie Mullan (13)
Gresham's Senior School

The Boy On A Bike

It must be pretty cool to be that boy
Sitting on his bike on a Monday morn
As we head off to school.

I wonder if his mum nagged him this morning
About not being awake in time
I bet he didn't have homework last night
And didn't have to be in bed at 10 o'clock
He probably stayed out all night
I wonder if it was cold
It might have even rained
Would he have been scared
Or perhaps even hungry?

A night must seem pretty long
On your own in the dark
A day must seem pretty long
With no mates to make your laugh
In fact, now I think about it,
He looks pretty lonely sitting there on his bike.

Jed Jordan (13)
Gresham's Senior School

To Jasrala With Love

Sinking slowly from the sad sunrise,
The battered buildings stand tall
Then their jagged forms crumble
Falling from the troubled sky to
Shattered bones, resting in piles.

Bodies lie beside them
Yet oblivious to the young girls' eyes
Their laughs are a torment
To the doomed innocent
And for each letter a life
Each word a family, the loving
Message of horror, a
Pen pal's letter, inscribed with foreign blood.

The warheads stand tall
Their Lebanese hatred now clear
Shimmering in the claustrophobic heat.

I watch this with a leadened heart
For I know that a bloody message, will
Eventually be signed for my fate.

Connie Birch (13)
Gresham's Senior School

Our World

If the world was flat
Not round;
Who would be the first
To fall off?

If one by one
We dropped
And fell through time
Where would we land?

If we lived forever
Never died
But still grew old
Would we enjoy it?

If we are stuck how we are
No change
And we are killing our world
Do we really care?

Roya Athill (13)
Gresham's Senior School

Baby

Whine, whine, cry, cry
Is it all they do?
Well no, not exactly
Unless they need the loo.

Waah, means hello
Cry! means goodbye
Gurgle means how are you?
And ga-ga means, why?

So when you see a baby
You'll listen to their sounds
You know what has been said
And you can understand.

Natasha Hailey (12)
Hethersett High School

Space

Space is covered in a veil of mystery
A journey through time itself
Black holes and meteorites clustered together
Like tools in a pitch-black shed.

Mercury, a scorching marble floating in space;
Venus, a silent twin sister;
Earth, a cloudy crystal suspended in the black;
Mars, a drop of blood caught in mid-air.

The asteroid belt is an unforgiving face,
Ordering living creatures to stay away
Rocks hurtle down onto foolish beings who ignore the warning.

Jupiter, a Mount Olympus for the gods of time and space;
Saturn, a Frisbee and ball welded together;
Uranus, a misty orb, glowing green;
Neptune, a great luminous sapphire;
Pluto, a chunk of granite millions of miles away from civilisation.

Yeah, space is a pretty spectacular place,
With the sun like a great glass dome,
But there's one place I'd rather be right now
And that one place is home.

Kieran Davis (12)
Hethersett High School

What Is Imagination?

Imagination is a leap down under
A beam of sunshine that shines down blinding you for a second
A horse that gallops past so fast you can't see it
A peacock full of colours
A bird that comes and goes, even stays a while
A rainbow full of thoughts.

Cami Bounden (12)
Hethersett High School

Sailing

Silently slicing through the shimmering sea
Tenderly tacking and turning with the tiller
Dancing dolphins darting beneath the dashing boat
Foaming froth following us towards the faint horizon
Benevolent breeze bustling from behind
Alone on an adventure awaiting and admiring what's ahead
Swooping seagulls circling serenely up above
Meandering onwards to the magical mystery.

Lily Lacey-Hastings (13)
Hethersett High School

Creation

On the first day God made parents
On the second day God made alcohol, beer, cider and vodka
On the third day God made vegetables
On the fourth day God made Ikea flat packs
On the fifth day God made rattly cars
On the sixth day God created clothes shops and saw that it was boring
On the seventh day He got out of bed the wrong side and
                                                    made children.

Jonathan Grainger (12)
Hethersett High School

The Sea

The swishing sea sunk the stranded sailor
The sounds of the whoosh and waves of the wonderful ocean
The swoop of the swishing sea
Beating the battered rocks on the beach
The cruel water crushing the cliff
The swishing whirlpool whirls and whirls
The terrifying sea is tremendous.

Daniel Tompson (12)
Hethersett High School

Creation

On the first day God made parents
On the second day God made money for the parents to buy stuff with
On the third day God made tea and coffee
And on the fourth day God made nightclubs for parents who like to let
their hair down
And God though parents should have something better
So He invented lush sofas and poufs so they could chill-out with Him
on the seventh day
On that day He was resting and set His alarm clock incorrectly
On waking God became restless -
It was then He made his first and only mistake - children.

Adam Browne (12)
Hethersett High School

Four Seasons

Oh beautiful spring
So happy the butterfly
Upon the nectar.

Up high in the sky
Do the young birds swoop and dive
On a summer's day.

On the autumn's ground
Lay mainly leaves red and brown
Hedgehogs huddled under.

The icy winds blow
Nothing hard nor seen above
Cold layers of snow.

Eleanor Gash (12)
Hethersett High School

My Rabbit

My rabbit sits all day in a flower bed like a fluffy, grey flower.
A lonely old spinster, she looks down her ever-twitching nose at us disapprovingly,
And kicking and snorting she bites the hand that feeds her, literally.
She chases the dog round the garden, but at least she cuts the weeds.
Queen of our garden, she knows how to get everything she needs
No one wants to feed her when we're on holiday.
She doesn't do hugs or cuddles -
But I love her anyway
Beware of the rabbit!

Verity Hemp (12)
Hethersett High School

Dear Forest And Ocean

Dear Forest,
We are the creatures that roam around you,
The birds that swoop above you
The campers that sleep among you
The nests that perch on you
And the sun that flies above you
Across the sky till nightfall.

Dear Ocean,
We are the fish that swim through your body
The rain that falls into your vast swelling waves
The fishing lines that grip your own sea life under the rippling foam
And the warming sun above your reflecting light.

Laura Butcher (12)
Hethersett High School

David Beckham

He is a fast Ferrari
He is a quick hummingbird
He is all over the place
He is a striking football trophy
He is a Saturday afternoon when the football is on
He is a wet, miserable, soggy morning
His football boots are as shiny as a window.

Gregory Drew (13)
Hethersett High School

Animals

Leaping laughing Labradors lick lollipops legally
Carpeting caring cheetahs collect coins cautiously
Fantasising far-reaching fish flinch ferociously
Radiating ruffling racoons ram-raid raspberry razors rapturously
Sizzling sacrificing salmon salivating satisfactorily
Hard hankering hares hassling head teachers hauntingly
Gorgeous grey gorillas gather grapes greedily
Bouncing baby bears buy black bananas belatedly.

Sam Rock (12)
Hethersett High School

Creation

On the first day God made teenagers
On the second day God made music and chocolate
On the third day God made the city
On the fourth day God made clothes, shoes and accessories
So we could look better
One day a teenage girl called Millie played Him up
So on the fifth day God made school!

Millie Yorke (12)
Hethersett High School

Where Do I Belong?

Where do I belong?
In the countryside, living on a farm,
With horses, dogs, pigs and tractors ploughing fields,
Quiet as a mouse, not a peep,
I often say to myself, where do I belong?

Where do I belong?
In the city, living in a terrace house,
With shops, pubs, nightclubs and kids in the park,
Noisy traffic at night, not a moment to think,
I often say to myself, where do I belong?

Where do I belong?
In the Australian outback, hot, living in scrubland,
With snakes, spiders, bugs, nothing apart from a desert,
Howling, chirruping, strange sounds in the dead of night,
I often say to myself, where do I belong?

Where do I belong?
In the Siberian tundra, cold, extreme weather conditions,
With snow, icicles, big skies, hardly any warmth,
The sound of teeth chattering together, day and night,
I often say to myself, where do I belong?

Where do I belong?
Not in any of these places, that's for sure,
I belong with my family, my dogs and my goldfish,
In my ex-RAF house, sufficient noise, time to think,
In Watton, that is where I belong!

Ursula Denson (13)
Hethersett Old Hall School

My Names

Becky, my other normal name
I don't like this one as much
Bexa, my cousin's, 'Hi, how are you?'
Beckah Boos, my annoying name, Nana's here.
Smiley Joe, my strange nickname!
Rebekah, oh no, I'm in trouble.
My name's my identity: change my name, change me.

Rebekah Oelrichs (11)
Hethersett Old Hall School

My Dad

My name is Stuart, I am 43 years old
One of my daughters thinks I am very old!

I have one sister, three children
A wife, mum and dad and two dogs
I like to think I am casual
I usually have a bad knee
And a bad back and psoriasis
Perhaps my daughter is right I am getting old!
I am medium height and a little bit round
My voice has got a London accent in it
I have a kind soft voice and hardly ever shout
I don't have much hair left and I am going grey
But what hair I do have is short
And I think I am tidy-looking
My thoughts are usually positive
I am usually happy
But I do get annoyed very easily
I barely ever shout
This is who I am!

Bethany Shearing (11)
Hethersett Old Hall School

My Identity

My name is Ellie and I'm small,
You'll know it's me 'cause I'm not tall.

I'm getting older, my age is eleven,
Chocolate and sweets are my idea of heaven.

My hair is brown, my skin is tanned,
I have bitten nails upon my hand.

I love to snuggle in my cosy bed,
My bedroom's great with walls of red.

I like to read and my favourite colour's white
In the wind you'll find me flying my kite.

You'll see me dressed in the latest fashion,
To me it's always been my passion.

I think I'm funny and can be rather loud,
I hope that I stand out in a crowd.

Ellie Davies (11)
Hethersett Old Hall School

Identity

What is an identity?

Is it your clothes?
But then no one knows where you live.
Is it your size?
But then no one knows your different emotions.
Is it the way you look at things?
But then no one knows your beliefs.
Is it your health?
But then no one knows your age.
Is it your colour?
But then no one knows your name.
Is it your name?
But isn't a name just a word people know you by?
It's not your personality.

Catherine O'Neill (11)
Hethersett Old Hall School

Names

A name is very important
Something that you have had forever
Something that you will have forever
No one can steal it away from you
You will have it all through childhood and adulthood
It can never be properly changed
The name that your parents have given you
Will never be stolen from you
Or snatched away at the dead of night
It is your most treasured possession.

Rose Herbert (11)
Hethersett Old Hall School

Identity

Identify me,
What is it you see?
On the surface I move and breathe like you,
But inside is where my identity grew.
My looks, my thoughts are unique to me,
On first meeting my looks are all that you see.
If you care to look deeper, to see what's inside,
Look into my eyes, they're open wide.
I am different from you and you from me,
We have our own identity.
I can laugh and cry and try my best,
But what makes me different from the rest?
Is it how I feel or speak or look?
Can you read me like a book?
What's inside and what you see,
Is what makes up my *identity!*

Abigail Ulrych (13)
Hethersett Old Hall School

Identity

I am unique, there's only one of me
D on't need to make anyone else happy but myself
E veryone's different
N othing you say will change me
T his is who I choose to be
I know who I am
T ime to show it off
Y oung and free.

Hannah Gowing (12)
Hethersett Old Hall School

Why Do We Have Flaws?

I am good at certain things,
I'm much better than you,
Yet you are good at things
I won't even try to do.

Why do we have flaws?

I could talk for hours and hours
And gabble even longer,
But when it comes to making sense,
It's clear that you're the stronger.

Why do we have flaws?

I'm sure that I can sing and chant
It gives me a big head
But when it's time for swimming,
I'm so bad, I drown instead.

Why do we have flaws?

So, why are we so good, yet bad?
Well, it's our identity.
It makes up who we are
And it defines you and me.

Madison-Mae Gianfrancesco (12)
Hethersett Old Hall School

What Shall I Wear Today?

What shall I wear today?
A purple and red top?
A pair of green trousers?
Should I look bright and flowery
Or tough and black?
But do I want to be seen as an individual
Or someone else?
How can I decide
There's so much in my wardrobe?

I feel gentle today
So I'll wear violet.
But I also feel energetic,
So should it be a bright pink, or blue or red?

What'll happen if I wear grey or white?
Will people treat me more gently or rough?
If I wear brown, will people think I'm shy
And I wonder what'll happen if I wear stripes?

Kim Hazell (11)
Hethersett Old Hall School

Identity!

Identity, identity, what is my identity?
I suppose my name,
My date of birth,
What I wear and how I look,
My fingerprints perhaps.
But I think the things that make me, me, are.
A walk on the beach, a swim in the sea,
A ride across the fields on a horse,
A laugh with my friends,
Some music,
And . . .
So much more that's *me!*

Hannah Gaskin (11)
Hethersett Old Hall School

Norwich

Bubbles blow down Gentleman's Walk
Pushy, arrogant businessmen,
No time to talk!

Young mothers with pushchairs
Just walk into you, clearly can't stop,
Just too much to do.

Chavs in miniskirts, fat and thin,
Look to what's on the outside,
Not within.

The elderly creep out of the woodwork,
To get in the way, can't miss out on shopping
On this fine Norwich day.

Toddlers heads are in the clouds,
Digging a path through the bustling crowds.
'Big Issue, Big Issue,' such passion
Such excitement in the salesman's voice
The longing in his eyes, gives you no choice.

Lap up the joy, hear the noise
Appreciate shop windows,
Lined with toys.

For soon it will be over and the chill will slip in
Through the city walls the heat will fade
And the leaves will fall.

Jasmine Philpott (13)
Hethersett Old Hall School

I Want To Be Myself Again

I can't remember how I changed,
All I know is that I hate it
And wish I could be myself again,
Can I do it?

Can I be myself again
The way I like to be?
I wish I could go back in time
And change back to my nicer self.

I feel like I can't remember my past,
As if it's been pushed out.
By my new self; the one I don't like
What is my identity?

I'm still the same on the outside,
But I've changed inside.
The one that really matters,
My personality.

I don't want your identity,
I have got mine,
I want to be me
And keep my identity!

Charlotte Bacon (12)
Hethersett Old Hall School

My Identity Poem

If I was a dog,
I would be a Labrador,
Friendly and loyal,
There for you when you want me!

If I was a cat,
I would be a tabby,
Not a posh cat,
But a normal laid-back one.

If I was a bird,
I would be a peacock,
Screaming at my sisters,
With bright colours and long hair!

If I was a sheep,
I would be a Jacob sheep,
Two different colours,
Not following the majority of the crowd.

If I was a horse,
I would be a wild stallion,
Wanting to run free in big meadows
And eating lots of long fresh grass.

Now you know my identity if I was an animal.

But, if I was an emotion,
I would be a smile,
Because smiles catch on
And so I would be up-to-date in fashion!

This is my identity,
I hope you agree with it,
Because this is me
And I am this and nothing can ever change it!

Claudia Grattan (12)
Hethersett Old Hall School

The Lady In The Mirror

Look at the mirror, what do you see?
A strange young woman looking back at me.

With dark black eyes
And tanned brown skin
Do they cover up lies
That add to your sins?

A dark lock of hair,
Falling over your face.
Have you something to hide
Are you living in disgrace?

That long pointed nose,
Casts a shadow on your cheek.
The shadow so dark,
Like a winter that's bleak.

Your rosy-red lips
And your teeth shining bright.
Those teeth like the moon,
Sparkling so white.

Those ears so long
And your voice so cold,
Like a haunted forest,
Forever cursed, old.

I'll tell you once more what I see in that glass,
A mysterious lady that's floating past.

Vicky Ramshaw (12)
Hethersett Old Hall School

What Is A Name?

A name is something very special,
It is individual and not always well known,
It is something that people recognise you by,
Something to call your own.

The first thing said when meeting new people,
Something shouted across a room,
It could be said in a sweet and gentle way,
Or bellowed in a voice of doom.

A name stays with you for the whole of your life,
Chosen before you were born,
It gets said so many times by all sorts of people,
But will never get old and worn.

It may be printed loudly on a name tag,
Or filed way down deep,
But no matter how much it is hidden or shown,
It will always be something to keep.

Chloe Lochhead (12)
Hethersett Old Hall School

Identity

If I would be a car I would be a Beetle.
Rolling along with vibrant flowers on my back.

If I were a flower I would be a sunflower
With my head held high in the sky.

If I were an animal I would be a monkey
Swinging from tree to tree, eating bananas as I go.

If I were a piece of clothing I would be a jumper
Making people feel warm and comfortable.

If I were a subject I would be maths
I can be complicated but also quite simple.

If I were a genre I would be fantasy
Some people find me fantastic, others don't.

If I were jewellery I would be a bracelet
I can be glamorous, but also quite plain.

Harriet Waring (12)
Hethersett Old Hall School

Who Am I?

Who am I?
Who am I?

I am like a dolphin flipping up and down.

Who am I?
Who am I?

I am like a little girl trotting up to town.

Who am I?
Who am I?

I am like a hyena giggling when I want.

Who am I?
Who am I?

I am like the computer always changing *font*.

Who am I?
Who am I?

I am like the sunshine, always smiling
And that's who I am!

Katie Nunney (12)
Hethersett Old Hall School

My Friend

So tall you stand, so proud and strong,
As you have stood all summer long,
So golden-brown, so blonde and fair,
The grains of corn are but a crown you wear.

As you bask in the dying sun
The insects buzz, you hear their song,
Suddenly a growl, a rumble deep
And from the shed a monster creeps.

There is no escape, you cannot run,
Your feet are too deep, your hope is gone.
The beast's body flashes red,
His teeth start spinning, he wants to be fed!

As careless as a summer breeze,
You're cut down with thoughtless ease.
The farmer sits upon his throne;
He has reaped from what he's sown.

No more I see your happy face,
No more the field blessed with grace,
Nature does as nature pleases;
But fond memories will never cease.

Francesca Warner (13)
Hethersett Old Hall School

Identity

I love my new dress.
It's so beautiful, the lady in the shop said it complimented my figure,
I think that's what she said, I can't really remember.
I'm meeting up with the girls so we can do some knitting
I'd better just check in the mirror, see if the jumper goes with the dress.

Staring back at me there is a thin old wrinkled face
Grey hair, dull skin
This isn't me, is it?
Who has stolen my fantastic looks?
My long golden hair
My perfect China-doll skin
What's happened?
I should go, seeing my friends will cheer me up.

Look at that old lady walking along the street
Grasping her knitting needles and handbag tight.
I wonder what she used to look like
We should stop staring or she might feel threatened.

Look at Gail, she looks so beautiful.
I love her new dress
Her hair is grey, her skin wrinkled, her handbag worn,
But to me she is beautiful and always will be.

Alice Baillie-Johnson (13)
Hethersett Old Hall School

My Invisible Identity

When I'm around family I am invisible,
When I'm around friends I am invisible,
When I'm around teachers I am invisible,
When I'm around me I am who I want to be.

Who I want to be is a person in my dreams;
I dream my family and friends can only see me,
I dream my teachers only ask me,
I dream I'm who I want to be.

When I'm in the cinema I am invisible
When I'm in the playground I am invisible,
When I'm in the shops I am invisible,
When I'm in my garden I am who I want to be.

When I'm in my garden there is only me,
I can scream to the top of the trees,
I can run as fast as the wind,
I can be who I want to be.

There is only one me and I am finally that person
Who can be noticed, when I scream to the top of the trees,
I am now who I want to be.

Camilla Carr (13)
Hethersett Old Hall School

School

School can be good, it can be rough on the field
School can be bad, it is gentle in class
Sometimes we have a laugh, so school is alright
Sometimes you'll get wrong if you are alright.

Simon Waterfall
Litcham High School

Beauty And The Beast

The man, gnarled and ugly
Shrivelled in a dark corner
Crumpled in a heap
As his stone heart
Thuds dully against his chest
Picking at a spot on his nose repeatedly
Pick, pick, like a grey prune groaning
And moaning to anyone who will listen
Ugly!

The woman, beautifully
Singing to an expectant crowd
Smiling her perfect smile
As a glow radiates from her angelic face
Prancing and dancing, her long blonde, flowing hair
Cascading behind her like a waterfall
Her sparkling blue eyes glancing around
As if she has not a care in the world
Her bubbly attitude filling the room with happiness
Beautiful!

Amy Lewins (11)
Litcham High School

Friend

Friend
Care, kind
Understanding, trusting, loving
Playmate, fond, special: opposition, inconsiderate, annoy
Rivalling, irritating, hounding
Loathe, despise,
Enemy.

Jernene Poponne (12)
Litcham High School

The Bully And The Victim

The bully,
The hunter of the school
Stalking the corridors
Homing in on the prey
Hatred coursing through him
Blue fire burns evilly in his eyes
The fire of Hell
The sun burns out
As he towers over his victim
A look of amusement on his face.

The victim,
Huddles in the corner
Whimpering like a dog
Anger and pain engulf him
So alone and petrified
Mentally scarred and feeling lousy
As the evil washes over him
Pulling him down
Down into the pit of Hell.

Sam Bates (11)
Litcham High School

Night-Time

It's dark and very, very quiet
Slowly the badgers creep out of their sett.
They sniff their way along their nightly path
To hunt for food on their nightly trek
An owl screeches up in the old oak tree
It's spotted a small movement, hopefully tea
A fox trots through the woodland path
But the rabbits scurry back down their holes
The deer grazed peacefully under the silver moonlight
Which softly lights up our room as we sleep through the night.

Ryan Pooley (11)
Litcham High School

All About Us

We have to look out for each other
To care and be kind
Our beautiful Earth is all for us
So don't be greedy
Through our time we're making the world a better place
It's always improving
So, why are we here?
We're here to save us from extinction.
So we don't all die out
To experience love
Having a relationship
To reproduce
Having children
And to learn
To improve every day
But all you have to remember is
Wherever you are
And whoever you are
We are all important.

Liam Reeve (11)
Litcham High School

Why?

Why are we here? Why?
Why are we on this planet? Why?
Why did we end up here?
Why did we not end up on Mars? Why?
We are here because God put us here
And I'm proud of it.

Conor Fraser (11)
Litcham High School

St George's Horse

S adness fills my heart
A covetous horse I am
I am jealous of George
N othing I do impresses him
T o be or not to be?

G eorge is a selfish man
E legant and experienced
O h what a beautiful maiden
R apid dragon
G raphic maiden eww!
E xcellent
S hire killer

H e is killed by George
O i, get off me
R ivals fought well
S tupid dragon
E vil has been defeated.

Ross Breedon (11)
Litcham High School

My Roast

Roast is my favourite food
I eat it when I get it
I will prefer a roast
Than a crumbly bit of toast.

Carrots, runner beans and peas
Are the bee's knees
And the broccoli
Is my little treat.

Curtis Hughes (11)
Litcham High School

Tree

For hundreds of years the old tree stood
Surrounded by friends in the Three Acre Wood.

It was peaceful, it was full of love
Small creatures lived below, birds soared above.

For many years it seemed that nothing could go wrong
But Man with hate and greed silenced birds in song.

Down they pulled the trees, away flew every bird
From miles around destruction could be heard.

And now alone stands that one tree, inside it's aching and crying
For all it can remember is . . . the image of fellow trees dying.

Rosanna Elliott (12)
Litcham High School

St George's Horse

S ometimes I'm the greatest of all
T oday is the day I am strong and powerful

G iving me the strength to be in a battle
E very time I have an instrument, it rattles and rattles
O verall I hold the instrument with my teeth
R acing St George as he is such a thief
G oing to say St George is like a skull-faced skeleton
E very day I wish he could get pecked by a pelican
S o today is the day that I am the greatest of all

H elp is what St George is saying
O verall to me he is dead and he is laying
R eigning to me is over the place
S ometimes it's annoying and it is such a disgrace
E very day he is putting me through such a pace.

Colleen Marsh
Litcham High School

St George's Horse

I am really huffy
I've got this great load on my back
Straining my backside down to the floor
Like a hundred tonne weight pulling me off a cliff
And that foolish artist made me look like a right old dope
With my legs kicked up to kingdom come
And my neck feels like a bowling alley
And then how do you think I felt
In front of this gutless dragon?
I am really huffy.

Luke Pratt (12)
Litcham High School

Bully

Bully
Rough, tough
Scaring, hurting, threatening
Mean, heartless, violent, scared, innocent, terrified
Trembling, crying, worrying
Petrified, fearful
Victim.

Victoria Rutterford (11)
Litcham High School

I Wish

I wish I was there right now
As I stand here, there are butterflies piercing through my heart
I hear the whistle blow
I must drag myself away from my own planet
In my mind where there is no prejudice, just peace
I snap back into existence
Fumbling legs
I throw him
Groping arms
I hold him
Fear in his eyes
I think to myself, *how can an enemy be scared*?
Wriggling body
Must stay strong
Petrified
Unwavering
Determined
Must keep firm
Clock ticks
Sweat pours
Losing grip
Losing all being
I want to go back
I am lost in my mind
I am running towards reality
That I cannot find. Help!

Nathan Woolley (14)
Taverham High School

Devil!

Red, red, red,
This is the colour of Hell
No cheery bells
Just witches' spells
And the Devil who lies within.

Orange, orange, orange,
This is the colour of Hell
A rocky terrain
Is causing a campaign
But not with the Devil who lies within.

Yellow, yellow, yellow,
This is the colour of Hell
Great pools of fire
Fit for a liar
Including the Devil within.

Red, orange, yellow
These are the colours of Hell
No happy soul is found in here
Except for the Devil who lies within.

Joely O'Brien (12)
Wymondham High School

Harmless

They were just sitting there
Doing no harm, just sitting there.

But someone had a grudge
A grudge that had to be settled.

They were just talking, playing games
Doing whatever they wanted.

He wasn't giving up, it had to be done
Nothing would stop him.

They got up and moved across the field
Then sat down again to talk to some other friends.

He took aim, one hit it would be over
No more worry.

Bang!

It struck
He fell to the floor, just a harmless group
Terrorised by one shot
Just harmless . . .

Scott Cogman (14)
Wymondham High School

Out Of My Window

Out of my window I see trees,
Tall ones, short ones,
Different shaped leaves,
All these trees dancing in the wind.

Out of my window I see a flower,
Tall, thin and purple,
Seems to grow an inch an hour,
The tall flower swaying in the breeze.

Out of my window I see grass,
Very short, very green,
I doubt that will last,
The short grass ripples in the wind.

Out of my window I see three rabbits,
Fun, but a bit fat,
Eating too much cabbage,
Their fur blows softly in the breeze.

Out of my window is my garden,
Small, but full,
All these things make up my garden,
Dancing together in the wind.

Becky Knivett (14)
Wymondham High School

The Red Ink

The red ink that flows
All thick and clotted as it runs
The drip, drip, drip as it drips on the floor
The tears seem to be unstoppable
The laughter that seems to have run dry
How long should we let it go on
Before we should say that's enough?
Who should be the one to make that decision?
Is it fair on all of the people who surround?
Whoever is there to protect and hold?

Hannah Harvey (15)
Wymondham High School

My Bright Hours Of Darkness

My head rested on the floor
One sound, that I heard before
There were echoes of small tunes, which lasted long,
I laid and listened to the crickets' song.

My feet rested in the cool
In the water, in the pool
It moved like silk, through my toes
I glanced up into the sky into my pose.

Stars glimmered and shone
All that time, for that long
They were diamonds scattered
Nothing no longer mattered.

A warm breeze combed my hair
My mind was some place, somewhere
As I lay, the hours passed
I wanted to stay, for it to last.

It was a calming cure
Of the mind I'm sure
This place that I do adore
Shall stay in my heart for evermore.

Kerry Leeds (14)
Wymondham High School

The Tramp

I used to see him every day,
In his expensive pinstripe suit,
Walking confidently to his office,
He would sit on his luxurious leather chair,
Behind his large oak desk,
Giving out orders and
Staring mindlessly into his computer screen.

Then I saw him every day,
Hunched in the doorway,
His old shaggy dog laid quietly at his cold feet,
The dog's grey muzzle,
Matched his master's grey beard,
His face sad and lifeless,
With a blank look on his face.

Now I see him every day,
Still hunched in the doorway,
But this time playing a sweet melody,
On his harmonica,
With his worn-out cap laid on the floor full of rusty coins,
His clothes were once designer
Now they are just rags
He used to have everything
Now he has nothing.

Rebecca Simpson (14)
Wymondham High School

Death

A high-pitched screech
Signalled her death,
Murmurs from doctors rushing
Around
Sobs wailed through the white walls,
Rebounding off the white walls and white floors,
The curtains draped
Across the lifeless body,
All colour had gone,
Her flesh still warm to touch,
But do I dare touch her?
Can I touch her?
Life feels so lonely,
A dark room has trapped me,
No one touches me,
Just whispers
Like I've gone as well,
Have I gone?
Will we meet again?

Hanna Jaggs (15)
Wymondham High School

Rotation

As you roll into the bank,
You feel the rush of excitement,
The momentum of that single push,
Puts you flying in the air,
The deck feels like it's stuck to your feet.

The judges were stunned,
Couldn't believe what you had just done,
The technicality of that trick
Was intense,
Everyone was speechless.

How could anyone think
That wood, wheels and metal combined,
Could turn into an amazing sport?
All your life people doubted you,
Your board if your life.

Your career is over,
But the passion is still there,
People still remember your skills,
You were a professional skateboarder.

Thomas Cuthbert (14)
Wymondham High School

Naughty Boys

Naughty boys
Get their way
Naughty boys
Should learn to pay

Naughty boys
Are never good
They never do
As they should

Naughty boys
Cry all night
They can't resist
To start a fight

They may be rough
They may be tough
But they need to know
That if they stay bad
They'll get a smack on the bum
From big mean Mum.

Andy Hatch (14)
Wymondham High School

The Field

A solitary oak,
Stands and stares
At the deep dark mud,
Barren and bare.

Under a powdery blanket,
That fell from the sky
Sleeping in silence,
A winter passes by.

Rays of warmth
Penetrate the earth
Delicate green shoots,
A miraculous birth.

Raindrops dance and jump,
The earth no longer dry
Tiny leaves stretch up,
Longingly to the sky.

Tall golden heads,
Stand proud in the field
Nearly time to gather,
This wonderful yield.

Matthew Smith (14)
Wymondham High School

Eternal

Sitting here just like anyone else,
But everyone seems to betray me.
I'm distant from here,
They just can't see it,
They don't know.

Every night since you left me,
To get a better view on life,
These tears have kept falling,
Your face in every one.

You didn't know I wanted you,
Never knew I cared.
You never knew I thought
Of you like that
Never knew I loved you.

Now sitting here like anyone else,
Thinking of what could have been.
I miss you and I'm reaching
Out for your hand,
To catch me as I fall as well.

Rebecca Everest (15)
Wymondham High School

Away With Words

In the hills of Scotland
There is a home
Deep in woodland
And if you lift a gnome
The wall splits in half
A passage leads down
Through a secret path
Under the ground!

There lives a person
Who's purely insane
Thinks he's an organ
With a yellow brain
But the oddest thing
Is the way he talks
He doesn't sing
Scream or squawk.

He speaks with rhyme
With stupendous rhythm
With interesting time
At any moment given
You could say he's cuckoo
All his ranting of words
But he's happy himself
Just away with words.

Thomas Ronan (12)
Wymondham High School

A World Of Misery

Born into a world of misery
Torn away from its mother
Drugged and caned
Hurt and lamed
This is the norm.
A horrible place
Full of waste
Burnt and bit
Kicked and hit
Dying is the norm.
Electrified
Not even at all
Shock to the head
Still being fed
Unhappiness is the norm.
Hung up by the leg
Cut off its head
Died in a world of misery
All for your pork pie.

Rebecca Greef (12)
Wymondham High School

A Nonsense Poem

A child on a swing with a sweet in her hand,
Throws it above, then it lands on the ground,
She gets up but finds it's cracked
Told her mum, but she got a big smack!

She got badly told off, but need not to worry
Her mum gave her a treat, a big bowl of curry.
She scoffed it all up in a bit of a flash
But to the toilet she had to dash.

She was happy again, sitting on her swing,
Eating some sweets and wearing some bling!
She dropped her sweets, but they didn't crack
All they did really was just smash!

Ruth Spurr (12)
Wymondham High School

Simple Honesty

You can be seen
But not heard
You can be in the spotlight
But feel in the dark.

And as you grow older
You learn that nothing is fair
And that the people in the world
Think only of themselves, they do not care.

Everything just carries on as normal
No one notices anything's wrong
And underneath that tough skin
Everyone's story is painful and long.

But then you come to realise
What's the point in trying?
Be happy, do your best
But inevitably you'll end up dying.

And as the world
Descends into darkness
Your life passes.

There's nothing in your mind
Apart from 'what ifs?'
Of how you truly feel
And after everything you go through in life
The end
Is just a simple and honest death.

Shoni Vaknin (13)
Wymondham High School

A New Star

I wish I was a brand new star
That could gaze upon the world from afar
In empty space
Which has no time, no rushed pace.

A bright new star with bright ideas
With no dilemmas and no tears
A clean blank page
That has no hatred, pain or signs of rage.

Emitting light to guide the way
Glad to have lived today
No opposition
Without rivalry, corruption, unfriendly competition.

A simple star in a bright blue sky
Something beautiful to the passers-by
Proud to be
As it is, what people see.

But I *am* a brand new star
I gaze at the bustling world from afar
It's cold out here, I'm all alone
I wish I lived on Earth
And had a home.

Eleanor Catherine (13)
Wymondham High School

Destitution

The once proud business man
Slouched in a bus shelter,
The six figure salary gone,
Life, wife and children lost.

Sharp, stylish suits are no longer,
Now just dirty, scruffy jeans.
The clean-shaven, smartly freshened look,
Replaced by weather-beaten stubble.

Grade II listed house, a distant memory,
Substituted by a run-down village shelter.
Flash cars and latest motorbike vanished,
Now only images in his head.

His past so bright, but future so bleak,
The hard work and success mean nothing.
The thriving business now bankrupt,
Leaving a desperate struggle to survive.

Izzy Roberts (14)
Wymondham High School

My Limerick

There once was a dwarf from Bell Air,
Who had some very weird hair
The hairdresser laughed
And they said she looked daft
As she looked like a big fuzzy bear.

Jessica Baker (13)
Wymondham High School

I Belong Here

Every morning and every evening
I begin to start believing
For the world I believe
And the people within
We should all hold hands and begin to sing.

For the family I love so dear
Everyone could see and hear
Our love will grow
Which will shine and show.

This land which we pray for and hold dear
The people inside will never fear.

As the magic within
The Kingdom of Heaven
I will always know I belong here.

Emma Lavery (13)
Wymondham High School

Stone Cold

S ad, hard, cold and helpless
T hat's what the dossers of London streets are like
O nly hope to get them through
N ever giving up
E verything that

C omes their way
O ffice work has been rejected
L ying in doorways to sleep at night
D ossing in the streets that's what we do.

Brogan Woods (14)
Wymondham High School

Roses Are Like Rainbows

Roses are many colours
More than I've ever seen
They come in many shapes and sizes
And this is just a dream!

Roses are like rainbows
Their colour shining bright
They brighten the darkest heart
Throughout the silent night.

Roses are like rainbows
Their colours will amaze
Any sad person
Throughout their lonely days.

Roses are like rainbows
They cheer up rainy days
They don't make you feel bad
They make you feel OK!

Catherine Buck (13)
Wymondham High School

The Bumblerone

As he lay in his bed and snored,
The Bumblerone was bored,
He hadn't any food,
All of it had been chewed,
He hadn't any drink
For he couldn't work the sink,
He hadn't any clothes,
As they're the things he loathes,
He hadn't anything to do,
He couldn't even reach the loo,
He had nothing at all,
Except his bed, so small,
So he lay in his bed and sighed,
Then, finally, he died!

William Oakes (13)
Wymondham High School

He

Obviously it's impossible for me to be in love
I mean, I don't even know him that well
But it feels so much more than infatuation
So much more than I'm willing to tell.

When I see him my insides turn over
I instantly begin to smile
I can't tear my eyes from his beautiful face
And walking towards him seems like a mile.

It's like I'll never get there
But when I do, it's all I hoped and more
He makes me laugh and sets my heart alight
Whenever I see him my jaw hits the floor.

I remain silent about my feelings
I long to whisper sweet nothings in his ear
I dream of holding him close
Of taking away his fear.

But this I know may never happen
It could but the chances are slim
Too much trouble lies in his waters
I long to reach his island, but I dare not swim.

Christina Websdale (13)
Wymondham High School

The Night

Miss McPherson is her name,
Poetry is her game,
A task she has set for me,
'Write me a poem Lewis but do it after tea.'

What kind of poem do I write?
Should it be about flowers, people or the night?
It seems to me the night is best
So I shall forget about the rest
My mind now will have to think
About the night as black as ink.

The daytime draws to a close and begins to fade
Then out come the stars that the good Lord made
I lie in my bed, my eyes closed tight,
Because I am afraid of the night.

Witches and demons come out to play
They don't fear the night, only the day
They come into the house, spreading their fear
I open my eyes they might see a tear
If they take me away it will be so sad
How I wish I could cuddle my dad.

It's not very nice being only three
Because everything at night scares me
When I am big and a great deal stronger
Afraid of the night, I won't be any longer.

Lewis Jolly (12)
Wymondham High School

My Culture

Life in the country is peaceful and quiet
Animals here and there and the odd deer in the field
Horses surround me and farms too
But who would know that just a car's drive away was a city
Large swarms of cars hover around the dull streets
And the buildings towering high above you
Loud noises and busy people
So much going on in such a little place.

Alex Stewart (14)
Wymondham High School

No More

As her tears fall to the floor
Happiness lives here no more.

Blissful memories of love not hate
The greedy demon killed, then hungrily ate.

His licking tongue of dark despair
Her terrified kin tried to run, somewhere.

But not here, no longer
As the demon grew, bigger, stronger.

The demon came, took her family, her place of love
She will see them no more, till in Heaven above.

The fire came and burnt all to the ground
Now she sits quiet, there is no sound.

The burning ashes at her side
She cannot be joyous, she's dying inside.

As her tears fall to the floor
Happiness lived here, but no more.

Jess Stratton (12)
Wymondham High School

Friends?

A word out of place,
The wrong conclusion drawn
Two sets of lips causing disgrace
Two pairs of eyes looking forlorn
Shouting and screaming
The quarrel goes on.

The teacher can't stop them
The parents fall out
By Monday morning
The children are full of doubt
'Why did we argue?'
They ask one another
On Tuesday afternoon
They are back together.

Victoria Cook (11)
Wymondham High School

I Love You

I love it when I'm with you
But when we're apart I cry
I think of you all day, non-stop
Then realise you're not here and sigh.

My feelings for you are so strong
Cannot describe what you mean to me
But now that we can't see each other
It's obviously not meant to be . . .

Never knew how it felt to be heartbroken
It'll take some time to mend
I will have to be careful next time
I give my heart to lend . . .

Lottie Penney (15)
Wymondham High School

Just For You

My heart is like a star or the sun
And it will not stop shining for you
I do not know what I have done
I can tell that this love is true.

I can't stand for us to be torn apart
I don't like the pain or the sorrow
It is time for us to depart
I know it won't come tomorrow.

My heart fits together like puzzled parts
Of my life with one piece that's missing
That piece breaks it, like poison darts
I will always think of us kissing.

I wish I could go back for a day
Just to hear your voice once again
But in my mind that's just a play
You stay in my head like a stain.

At night I cry out for you and your look
When I sleep, I sleep in sadness
You only exist in my sketchbook
Your melting look is my weakness.

Nicola Davies (11)
Wymondham High School

My Sub Culture

Turn the music up loud and let's copy our idols
(Kohl-rim our eyes
And dye our hair black)

Stand out in a crowd, let's use nicknames as titles
Stare at the sky
Till we're breaking our backs

Hang out in the bars and the clubs of our scene
Headbang at gigs
Where the singer just screams

Learn lyrics of songs - and know just what they mean
Jump up and down
With our sweet teenage dreams

Pierce our lips, our noses and ears
And show this dark world
That we have no fears

Develop opinions and stick to our guns
Growing up quickly
But still having fun.

Catherine Farrar (15)
Wymondham High School

Think Of A World

Think of a world without trees,
With no life in the seas,
A massive expanse with nothing living,
Nothing growing, no life giving.

A world once where there was green,
Birds flew in the sky to be seen.
People and animals, a happy band,
Inhabited this once fertile land.

Where there were forests that life gave,
Now nothing more than a grave.
Acid fumes and dirty smoke,
All of nature did they choke.

But it is today our concern
Mighty rainforests do we burn.
All to fuel Man's wanton greed
Never a thought to plant a seed.

Mother Earth is not ours to destroy,
But for all of nature to enjoy.
It is to the Earth we belong
We must protect before all is gone.

Abel Cater (14)
Wymondham High School

Colours Of The World

Look around at the grass so green,
Making up the beautiful scene.
Look around at the light blue sky,
Doesn't it make you want to ask why?

Why is the sky up there so blue?
Why do dogs bark and cows moo?
Why didn't God make us black and white?
Why does the fiery sun give us light?

Why is our hair all different shades?
Why do waterfalls fall in cascades?
Why do the peas that Lizzie hates
Come out of pods and end up on our plates?

We all have different colour skin,
Why should that change who we are within?
Why should we think of different scenes,
With daring heroes and evil fiends?

Look around at the grass so green,
Making up the beautiful scene.
Look around at the light blue sky,
Doesn't it make you want to ask why?

Anna Wyatt (12)
Wymondham High School

Her

Her face is like a goddess
Her eyes are like jewels
Her lips are soft like a pillow
Her touch is like an angel
Her voice is as sweet as love
Her hair shines like silk
Her kiss is out of this world.

This girl is the one you love
The one you will respect
The one that'll make you happy
The one you'll care for, for the rest of your life
The one you'll never forget.

Always be faithful
Always be there by her side
Treat her with respect
Never hurt her in any way
This person is your life, don't ruin what you've got.

Grady Woods (16)
Wymondham High School

Without Trust

For a while they are truly happy
Having fun, laughing, joking
Like a couple should
But then
People see how much their love is growing
How content and perfect they are
But eyes stray
Jealousy sets in
It doesn't take long
Before the trust has gone
And without trust
There is no love.

Alice Knights (14)
Wymondham High School

My Life

My life is a canvas
On which I will draw
My experiences are black, white, green or more.

My life is a bird,
That has not yet sung,
It hasn't decided how to use its tongue.

My life is a friend
That lasts forever
Through the good and the bad
It's there; whenever.

My life is a choice
The choice I have made
My life is a poker game
The card I haven't played.

People are sure they know what is best
But I know there is more, my relentless quest
And until that day
I will imagine and dream,
Plan and plot, aspire and scheme.

I only have one canvas
Completely unique.
I need to be careful
And think when I speak.
I must choose wisely
And take the right course,
Before my canvas is ripped
Stolen by force.

Rachel Wall (13)
Wymondham High School

Red Soldiers

All standing in line
Waiting for a sign
To charge for all good reasons
To not would be treason.

In our uniforms of red, we dread
Comforting clothes for the dead.

For the horrible moment we wait
For an outcome to decide our fate.

Bullet holes mark fierce fights
To victory that is within our sights.

We wait for the guns to stall
But we the red soldiers still stand tall.

Our hopes they are near
But we have to cross the clear.

To our families who love us dear
We fight for them, no fear.

Tom Mellor (15)
Wymondham High School

Having A Friend Like You

Having a friend like you
Someone who really cares
Someone to have a laugh with
Someone who's always there.

Having a friend like you
Who helps me when I call
Someone there to cry too
And say, 'I feel I'm going to fall.'

Having a friend like you
Who always helps and shares,
No matter what we've been through
We often share a tear.

Having a friend like you
There until the end
I just want to thank you
For being the best friend!

Rebecca Harris (15)
Wymondham High School

Friends

Friends are like stars
Lots of them around
Friends cheer you up
When you feel down.

Real friends will help you out
They know what you're about
And if they're there to the end
That's what I call a real friend.

Friends are also known as mates
Help you with boys, make mistakes
Always there to have a laugh
All the memories in one photograph.

Clare Vivian (15)
Wymondham High School

Sailing

I haul the sheets in, the sail tightens
The boat tips ever so slightly, balancing on the waves
The bow cuts through the rushing water like a biblical parting
The mast bends like a thin tree blowing in a gale
Rounding the last mark the boom flies over my head
I haul the sheets in, the sail tightens
The finish line is in sight.

Tim Mellor (15)
Wymondham High School

Inside The Box

Each day delivers new opportunities
Opens new doors, generates the desire for more

Each day unlocks new potential
As technology continues to prevail

Each week sees the bustle
Of the world of work

Each year we celebrate
The gain of more

And the whole time
Each day, each year

We keep ourselves
In the dark

Inside the box
Unaware
Of what really goes on outside.

Tom Wadlow (15)
Wymondham High School

The Countryside

The light is like a whirlpool of joy,
The clean fresh air is smothered in a cheery, hopeful,
                                    optimistic ambience
And the whole countryside is swarmed with glimmering beauty.
As the gentle teardrops of the sky linger down,
Tiny ringlets of wandering water expand into the tranquil streams
                                    of the lake.
The blooming flowers lunge their thirsty leaves at the passing dribbles
                                    of diving water
As the schizophrenic sun recessively pounds on.
The hospitable people stretch a smile to everyone that strolls past.
Happiness and contentment spreads through the countryside
Like a dominant wave of emotion.
That is until the dark comes to visit
When the dark comes, the curtain of light is closed and the
                                    darkness prevails.

The dark is like a vicious rush of poison circling, awaiting its prey
In the murky smouldering alleyways
Waiting to pounce on the vulnerable creatures
That are unfortunate enough to get in its way
The dark is like a cloud of pessimistic emotions conjured together
Creating a deadly combination of everything bad.

As you tiptoe through the dark roads, the trees' bony, cold fingers
                                    reach out
To grab you and the whistling wind violently swarms in your hair
                                    and against your body
Illusions of sinister shadows suddenly appear, knocking you into
                                    a tide of paranoia.

The hard thing is waiting for the light to come back
Until then, the unmerciful dark strolls the countryside, awaiting its
                                    next victim.

Alice Clarke (14)
Wymondham High School

My Culture Christmas

Children eagerly unwrap their presents
Tearing at the paper like hungry lions
Ripping it to shreds
To get at the golden treasures inside
Festive music plays in the background
And the walls reflect the tiny twinkles
Of the fairy lights in the tree
Everyone is happy at this time of year
Adults are laughing and joking
There is wine and crisps and chocolates to fill up on
When lunch is ready no one is really hungry
But they all flock to the table
Ready to stuff themselves as full as possible with all the lovely food
Bang! The first cracker is pulled
And everyone is shouting to be heard
Above the racket of the family
Later, there is more music and games
And then all are off to bed
The festive spirit won't last long
Soon the miserable looks
Are back on the tired faces of the adults
And it's back to work and school like normal
Until Christmas comes again.

Megan Hornby (14)
Wymondham High School

Our World

Our world is totally different to how it used to be
The world has changed as we have evolved.
Our culture is totally different to everyone else's on the planet
Our culture is mainly religion.

We have evolved with technology
As it has been produced and manufactured
But some countries in the world do not have these modern uses
                                        that we have

Some of them don't even have electricity.

There is no shortage of water here
But in places like Africa there is always a shortage of water in some
                                        of their countries.

We are not like animals prowling in the desert in search of water
Like some people are in the world that we live in.

I think that we are very lucky to live in our part of the world
Because otherwise there would be a lot more unhappy people
                            around in the society around us.

We do bear some similarities towards other countries
But our society is so different from theirs
Some people are animals fighting over which culture
And which part of the world that they want to live in
Even in some of our countries the societies are different
From the country that we live in today.

Megan Howard (14)
Wymondham High School

Take Over

A thousand buildings
Towering high
Offices, shops, schools
Our world is surrounded in grey
A busy life
No time to stop

People stressed
Food that they eat is unhealthy
They don't have time to cook properly
No fresh air or relaxation
Never stopping, work and social lives
Take over

That seems far, far away, but just out of the city
Lies a different world, different people, a different life.

Green and brown fields surround a tiny village
A few buildings
A church, a shop, a school, a pub
People have a community spirit
Children playing in the street until the sun sets
An easy life

A quiet area
A clean environment, fresh minds
Farmers drive over acres of land in tractors
That's the only sound to be heard for miles
Trees are plenty, sweet scents of flowers fill the air
A place to be proud of

The people in the city envy the villagers
If only they could lead such a peaceful life
But that's how people today live.
A split culture.

Camilla Jones (14)
Wymondham High School

Commercialised Christmas?

Around the fire at Christmas
The merry fire crackling
The crisp snow of celebration
The sharp frost of commercialisation.

The Christmas tree in Trafalgar Square
The gleaming lights of celebration
The dead branches of commercialisation.

Singing santas in the shop, their merry tune echoes
The chirrup of celebration
The beard of commercialisation.

Carol-singers at the door, mince pies for one and all
The warmth of celebration
The 'red nose' of commercialisation.

Gatherers outside the church, their gleeful chatter resounds
The Saviour of the world is born
The bringer of celebration.

Fay Johnston (14)
Wymondham High School

Stone Cold

S tormy and raining
T rying to go to job interviews, being a trainee
O rdure from the dossers and tramps
N agging people, finding a different way to camp
E verything is going wrong with me and Ginger

C rying, people think that I'm a minger
O ld-looking and scruffy
L ucky? More like very unlucky
D awn breaks, I want to go where it's warm.

Dominique Mutten (13)
Wymondham High School

My Room

When I walk in my room I always feel safe
The broad window shows the freedom outside
The real world I will soon enter.
I hear the faint humming like a bee
Do not be afraid, it's only the fridge
The wardrobe towers over me like a giant
However, it still enables me to take the items within
The metallic box resting on my small side table
Which indeed is my sound system
Allowing me to listen to my music
From rock to rap, hip-hop to pop whatever I like
The old toys I played with when I was young
Imprisoned in boxes, waiting for dust to bury them
My collection of multicoloured bouncy balls
Luminates my room every time I open the container
The magic ignites the room in seconds
The variety of posters on my wall
Makes me happy when I am feeling glum
The wall with its ocean-coloured looks
Reminds me of my happier times at the beach
Then my door, the only security guard
Allowing me to enter and leave my room
It has no emotion in its white textured look
My door is my only protection.

Greg Sheldrake (14)
Wymondham High School

Careless Community

House upon house upon house,
Water and money aplenty,
Electricity, food and gas,
Not a single stomach left empty.

People with jobs and health care,
Water, food and supplies,
Children with health and a future,
In our town, not a surprise.

No starvation, no droughts,
No financial problems.

Everyone secure,
Safety not a problem.

People living in luxury,
Money not a problem.

People throwing away food,
Hunger not a problem.

In our modern day society,
These things taken for granted,
So imagine living in poverty
An epidemic has landed.

Earth is filled with famine,
Poverty and disaster.

Earth is filled with famine,
Poverty and disaster.

Earth is filled with famine,
Poverty and disaster!

David Mayes (14)
Wymondham High School

Faster

Gun sounds
Adrenaline kicks
Legs move faster

Coach encourages
Crowd supports
Legs move faster

Getting raised
Lifted to the finish
Legs move faster

Pain digs in
Overwhelming agony
Legs move faster

Final few strides
Hands in air
Legs slow down

Goals accomplished
Legs slow down

Ambitions achieved
Legs slow down

What now?
Legs stop.

James Senior (14)
Wymondham High School

Shards Of A Broken Culture

Let's sit in silence
As we talk and we talk
Surrounded by people
And the view out is stark
Sky filled with smoke
And the pavement is hard
Glass hits the tarmac
Will pierce you with shards

Blend into the crowd
Like a cricket in grass
Or stand out against others
And the wind will be harsh
The light of the day will dwindle at dusk
And out come the girls of the night in the musk

Tea parties by TV
Ignoring the truth
These shards of a culture will form something new.

Holly Brearley (14)
Wymondham High School

Old Age

Sitting on the bench
My old bones creaking
Watching the fast-paced world go by
Wondering where my time has gone
It seems only yesterday
I was a young lad
Playing in the park
Looking at the old men on this bench
Thinking how I would never be like that
But here I am
The old man on the bench
Watching the world go by.

Kiara Jackson (13)
Wymondham High School

What Is?

What is love
But a tingle in the stomach
A beat in the heart
A twinkle in the eyes.

What is music
But a feeling in my stomach
A place in my heart
A space in my eyes.

What is money
But some cash in my hand
A jingle in my purse
A wedge in my pocket.

What are friends
Friends are everything.

Rachel Lambert (13)
Wymondham High School

Happiness

Happiness is a smile away
You'll find that out one day
There's always a smile
If you haven't had one for a while.

Always on someone's face
A twinkle in someone's eye
A dimple in someone's cheek
And a sparkle in someone's wine.

Happiness is always around
Somewhere, everywhere
'Tis always bound
And is never found
Where you suspect it to be round you.

Becci Cantle (13)
Wymondham High School

Stone Cold

S ad, scared and worried
T otally lost and confused
O nly thinking of the unhappy next day
N ever-ending with miserable life
E verything gets worse and worse

C old and depressed
O ngoing, never stopping unhappiness
L ong-suffering with sadness
D im life with nothing to look forward to.

Kasha Smith (13)
Wymondham High School

Wild Monday

The stampede of animals
Racing in the morning rush

The hyena's menacing laugh
At the spots dotted on your face

The eagle's digging in
At the deep-fried batter

The lead wolf howling
At the yawning crowd

The slippery serpent
Spitting on your homework

The tired blue whale
Floating around the Waitrose aisles

The warthog grunting
At you in your office chair

And the drowsy puppy
Watching 'Holby City'.

Amanda Tooke (15)
Wymondham High School

The Examination

First they make us study hard
Then march us into the hall
A smell of new paper, can be smelt
And the sight of the desk makes you quiver

They sit us down
Silence, across the room
Nothing is heard
Nothing at all

A scratching of rubbers
Marking of pens
Takes your mind off the question
Then you look at it and go mad
Saying you have done bad

You are sweaty, hot and clammy
You can't say, 'No more.'

When the bell goes you are not done
You think you are dumb
But who are you to know
The results are to judge.

You just wait for the results.

Jack Hornby (13)
Wymondham High School

I Wish . . .

I wish everyone could get along,
No more fighting, no more cries.
Where everyone is happy,
No more cheating, no more lies.

I wish people could share their love
Don't be mean, don't be sad.
We should all be treated the same
Don't be unfair, don't be bad.

I wish nobody would judge you,
By your actions, by your looks, by anything about you,
You should respect other people's feelings,
People would smile more and respect you too.

I wish wishes came true,
For you, for me.
Life would be so much better
And a happier place to be!

Lauren Webster (13)
Wymondham High School

Stone Cold

S topping and starting, meeting and losing people
T orturing hours of the night only leading to another
O nly myself to think about
N obody cares but me
E verything around me has collapsed

C old lonely nights
O nly myself to talk to
L ingering in only what seems to be
D arkness.

David Barber (13)
Wymondham High School

Summer

There's laughter and smiles in the atmosphere,
As the children rejoice that it's summer.
'Yes! No more school for six weeks,'
They shout with grins spreading to their cheeks.

The sun shines brightly in the far-off sky
And people gaze at the aeroplanes flying by,
Thinking back to their enjoyable vacations,
All those different tropical destinations!

In every garden there's meat sizzling
On the barbecues and champagne fizzing.
The adults are mingling politely,
While the children are playing brightly.

All the beaches packed to the brim
And more are in the sea having a swim.
Happy young ones digging around in the sand,
Peaceful old ones relaxed, hoping to get tanned.

Amy Richards (13)
Wymondham High School

What Is The World Coming To?

Every day I see cars with their smoky tail pipes
And the way that we are always told
To try and be energy efficient
Is imprinted in my brain now and forever.

We're using oil fifty times faster than we
Would have done fifty years ago
And petrol prices are so high that
No one can afford them anymore.

There are now so many roads
Leading to different places all over the country
That you have to use a GPS system
To avoid getting lost.

Is this the way we should live in the world?
Held back by restrictions on what we can/can't do?
One day we will run out of fossil fuels and
The world will be at a complete standstill.

Then, and just then, someone might stop and think -
Oh perhaps we should have done . . .

Lawrence Harmer (13)
Wymondham High School

Homework Lies

The teacher said, 'Where's your homework Fay?'
To be honest I didn't know what to say!

I hadn't been doing my homework you see,
I'd been sitting, eating and watching TV.

But I said, 'The dog stood on it with its muddy paws,
Then the cat came along, after showing off its claws . . .

He shredded it to pieces, there was nothing I could do.
I kept shouting at the cat, till my face went blue.

I decided I'd be good and copy it out again
But after looking around the house I couldn't find a pen.

So you see Mrs Peters that's the reason why,
I couldn't do my homework, I swear it's not a lie!'

I stood there waiting for what she was going to say,
But she didn't believe me about what happened yesterday.

She said, 'I'm disappointed Fay, for you to lie to me like that
To tell me this silly story about your dog and your cat.'

So thanks to me and my big mouth, I'm now writing lines,
I have to write, *I must not tell lies* more than 50 times!

Grace Parry (13)
Wymondham High School

Living In The 90s

Looking back on the memories,
I think how easy everything was.
Being a kid was really fun,
It was great living in the 90s.

Let's go back,
About ten years,
Let's think about it,
What we used to do,
How we used to be,
How we didn't have a care in the world.

When little girls would dress how they wanted
And playing armies in the fields was cool.
Playing hide-and-seek at dusk
And wearing arm bands to swim in the pool.

When we used to watch Rosie and Jim
The adventures of Winnie the Pooh
Tots TV, Hey Arnold and all the rest
Playdays and Ren and Stimpy too.

When Christmas was really exciting
And Santa came to see us.
We'd write out letters and be really good
And go to bed without any fuss.

But now ten years on,
Life seems so much more
Make-up, boys and all that stuff,
School and homework, such a bore . . .

Sometimes I wish I could go back a few years
And do all those things again,
Cos back then life seemed so much better,
What fun it was to live in the 90s.

Danielle Walpole (13)
Wymondham High School

The Jag

The purr of the car gave a punch and a pound
It got the speed onto the road
The steering was smooth and could turn very quick
Just what it needed to kill.

It pounded on its prize, he was panting very fast
He gobbled as the blood gushed out
It came low on fuel, he needed to drink
The water station is where he went.

He's out again, he thought it was a game
Until he heard the sirens and the fire
They had to stop, still it's worth a try
He went straight into the heat.

When he came through they were waiting right there
Waiting with guns held high
He turned back round but now he was trapped
There was only one thing to do.

He accelerated quick, heading right for them
They cleared as he went right past
He didn't stop, when he wanted to drop
He carried on into the mist.

The place was alerted, they knew he was coming
And they were hungry for meat
He knew he couldn't stop and he knew he would drop
Especially when the soul was shot.

Adam Latham (13)
Wymondham High School

154

Young Writers - Away With Words Norfolk

What's In My Pocket?

What's in my pocket?
I really want to see
Hopefully some chewing gum
Or a pebble from the sea.

What's in my pocket?
Something yellow or green?
Something I recognise
Or something I've never seen?

What's in my pocket?
Do I really care?
Maybe something worthless
Or maybe something rare?

What's in my pocket?
I'm going to see
Here I go, there's nothing
I tricked you, *hee-hee!*

Tom Morris (14)
Wymondham High School

They Don't Have A Clue!

A sad girl sits in the corner,
Wondering what will happen to her
She stares into space with a hopeless look in her eyes,
Thinking what will happen if her mum dies,
Her mum had a bad disease,
She begged the doctors to cure her please,
Tears began to roll down her cheeks,
All her friends said her family were freaks,
Little did they know the tears she cried
And no matter how hard she tried,
She couldn't get rid of the thoughts of losing her beloved mother.

Philippa Fromm (13)
Wymondham High School

Sam, The Boy Who Jumped On His Bed For Fun

There was a boy called Sam
His dad was a rather tall man
Sam was always on his bed
Jumping up and banging his head.

But one day, late at night
He gave himself a terrible fright
When the bed gave way
And he did pay as he had to sleep on the floor that day.

And after that fateful day
He never slept a wink
Because of the terrible stink
That arose from the floor and under the door.

After the inconsiderable pain
He apologised in total vain
But to very little avail
Because he still had the stink to inhale.

James Barrett (13)
Wymondham High School

My Last Words

These are my last words my darling love,
Waiting here to die and leave for above
If anyone asks I will be true
That this is how I want to go, dying for you
Be quiet my love, don't worry for me
Go on with your life, happy you must be.
Do not forget me, but do not mourn
Care well for our child, when he is born.
I feel my life coming to a short end
In my life's journey, this is just a bend
I will love you my darling, with all of my heart
Why, oh why do we have to part?

Luke Kennett (15)
Wymondham High School

When Will The Sun Come Out?

Howling sea,
Moaning people,
Violent gusts of wind, screaming vicious alerts of danger,
Leaping, rolling waves
Wailing, tossing, screaming,
Devastated people being drenched by the ocean,
Small, innocent children sobbing with every breath,
No lifeboats in sight,
Heaving rocks,
Boats drowning,
No food to eat,
No people to talk to,
You'd wish you were at home,
It feels like the storm of life will never be over.

Holly Hunter (13)
Wymondham High School

My Pre-Golf Shot Routine

First of all I select which club to use,
That can sometimes be tricky,
Next I have a practise swing,
That's the easy part,
Then I check the wind direction,
I see if it'll affect the shot,
I pick what to aim for in the distance,
That makes it much easier,
After that I step up to the ball,
Next I sort out my posture,
Then I take the club back
And hit the best shot I've ever hit!

Josh Bartlett (13)
Wymondham High School

My Life

What is the point of life?
Is it to conquer and win
Or is it to do your best
Maybe achieve and go on to better things?

But one thing's for sure
It is a journey with
A beginning, middle
And an end; death.

But in my life I have
Gone through all types of emotions
Love, joy, anger and pain
Love for my family.

Pain for losses
Anger with people
Excitement in danger
And laughter at jokes.

But in life you have
To be an individual
As that's what makes people
Themselves and unique.

Life is a gift and it should
Not be taken from an
Individual for any reason
We are lucky to live life.

We are lucky to be
Able to live life as we
Do in comfort and
Without disabilities.

Jonathan Walton (13)
Wymondham High School

The Ghost

Under the mysterious, misty moonlight stood a great ghost
White as a sheet, groaning gruffly
As he walked along the shingle in the driveway
As he swiftly swooped along the surface of the shingle
His chains clanked and clinked.

His red eyes gleaming with terror
That would scare the living daylights out of you
His chalk-white body
His whispering voice that weirdly enough is loud!

Bang, bang, bang went the blood-red door
It opened with a slow creak
He glided in
'Run for your life,' he whispered loudly.

Elly Mickelburgh (13)
Wymondham High School

Battlefield

I was down in a foxhole,
Our army on one side and the enemy in the other.
Bullets flying everywhere,
A hailstorm of mortar shells destroying the hillside.

No one side winning,
Everyone as scared as each other.
Then came the call,
The call to charge.

Our army got up and sprinted over the hill,
All falling down.
Bang . . . I look down and see a red stomach,
Then I fall down never to hear a sound.

Laurence Boulter (13)
Wymondham High School

Computer Graphics Becoming True

The stench of terrifying death in the air
Sights you just can't bear
Computer graphics becoming true
To helpless people like children in Iraq or you!
The gunfire echoing loudly in your room
But children in Iraq hear the real *boom!*
As one is dying in Iraq, the other one mocks
Punches and kicks, attacks him in flocks
The trigger being pulled
Your triangle button being pressed
Wounded, pleading, beside demolished houses.
'But I've only played the PlayStation a couple of hours.'
It doesn't take long for you to see
These graphics are becoming reality.
You play these games, you find it fun
But other children have nowhere to run.
The thoughts and feelings don't plummet in
To the place, deep within
Until they think it's okay to not let a human live another day
They'll kill, they'll murder, but get away
The images on the screen do come true
If you let them control you
So how about you play football outside today?

Elizabeth Fox (12)
Wymondham High School

Perfect

The media portrays the perfect woman,
A picture of an artificial angel,
Half plastic, half silicon,
A girl looks down at the image wondering why,
She's told to be thankful,
That she's got what she's got,
And to pray that she never gets old or ugly
Compared to the picture, she is grotesque,
Or so she thinks.

She has all the things someone wants,
She has all the looks someone wants,
She has the personality someone wants
And someone fell in love with her.

When she cries,
They do,
When she smiles,
Their heart skips a beat,
But she'll never realise that she's perfection in his eyes.

Eleanor Green (14)
Wymondham High School

Money, Money, Money

Money, money, money
It's all very nice
Money, money, money
You can buy expensive ice
Money, money, money
It makes you very rich
Money, money, money
But turns you into a witch
Money, money, money
You can go shopping every day
Money, money, money
It doesn't matter how much because you can pay
Money, money, money
Family gets great treats
Money, money, money
Move them to a better street
Money, money, money
Go on fab holidays
Money, money, money
Just sit there chatting all day
It's all about the money.

Rebecca Hawes (15)
Wymondham High School

Tropical Land

Sun glistening on the sea
Sand as white as a ghost
Palm trees as tall as skyscrapers
This is my perfect place.

Sun beaming down
On a deserted beach
No hustle or bustle
Just silence
This is my perfect place.

As I lie calmly on the sand
The sea crashing against the rocks
With a cocktail in my hand
My friends close by
This is my perfect place.

As the sun sets on my perfect place
The sky is orange
And I begin to wake
I roll out of bed
To start my new life
Is this really my perfect place?

Nicole Stevenson (15)
Wymondham High School

Designer Goods

It's a chavved up life
Always got a knife
Hang around the shop
Been around the block
Not much to do
Ain't got a clue
Got shouted at today in class
That teacher a right arse
Wearing all my bling
Can't afford a thing
But I'll get by
I'm always high.
My big gold hoops
Hanging from my ears
I ain't got no fears
Mess with me
You mess with my peers
It's just a chavved up life
Innit?

Kerri Notman (15)
Wymondham High School

Love

Love is a feeling
Like your heart peeling
Waiting for that special person
Love isn't real
Just something you feel
People think they're in love
When really it's a feeling from above
Hoping and waiting
Spend your whole life anticipating
Don't know what to say
This is just my way.

Chloe Priest (15)
Wymondham High School

Hallowe'en

More, more, more they chant,
Just waiting for the grant,
To stuff their pockets full of sweets
And to grab as many treats
As they can.

They go around in swarms,
Going over dew-covered lawns,
Just searching, searching, searching,
A little old widow, unsuspecting,
the fright,
That might
Stop her frail heart for a beat,
Just long enough to grab a treat.

The costume used last year,
That struck the fear
Into no one
But his pretending mum.

Up comes the sun,
Ending the fun,
Of a night,
That might
Be the worst in the year,
For that little dear,
Who lives . . . all alone?

David Mackenzie (14)
Wymondham High School

Fun

Fun
What we want
But
You must
Run, work, meet
Then
Fun
Always rushing
Phoning
Connecting
Running
Searching
Typing
All for
Fun
It's gone in a blur
Then home
But still connecting
Typing
Waiting,
Dialling,
Rushing
But it's
Fun
All for
Fun
And finally
The fun's there
Fun!
Yes!5
But in a second
It's gone.

Yolande Southgate (14)
Wymondham High School

Young Writers Information

We hope you have enjoyed reading this book - and that you will continue to enjoy it in the coming years.

If you like reading and writing poetry drop us a line, or give us a call, and we'll send you a free information pack.

Alternatively if you would like to order further copies of this book or any of our other titles, then please give us a call or log onto our website at www.youngwriters.co.uk

**Young Writers Information
Remus House
Coltsfoot Drive
Peterborough
PE2 9JX**

(01733) 890066